Moving marketing
from a perceived cost centre
into a strategic driver of profit

MARKETING:

THE
B⬤TT◎M
LIN£

ISBN: 978-1-7397820-0-9 (hardback edition)

Published in the United Kingdom in February 2022 by RJH Publishing

www.marketingthebottomline.co.uk

First, huge thanks to my brilliant mum and dad...
of course. You have shown me that hard work pays
off; you let me F*** up just the right amount, and,
somehow, you managed to rein in my (sometimes
outrageous) ambitions perfectly. I'm sure there were
times you doubted it was possible when I skipped
out of the Sixth Form to work in a pub, but, look...
I've written a book!

And to Bethany and Rory, thank you for always being
there. You have, genuinely, been the prevailing light
throughout the most stressful period of my life. You
are my life force and reason to succeed (especially
you, Bethany), and without you both to come home
to, I'm pretty confident I would never be able to
hold down a 'proper job'.

Iain and Tim, heartfelt thanks for providing me
with the opportunity to start my career at a young
age. Your incredible advice and guiding voices of
experience should be compulsory for every young
professional at the start of their career!

Finally, thanks to everyone who has worked so
tirelessly to help make alan. agency what it is today.
We are building a tremendously formidable B2B
agency, and I feel so privileged to work with such
a talented bunch of people day-in-day-out.
Seriously, thank you.

FOREWORD

Thomas Brown is a freelance journalist and reporter, award-winning author and independent consultant, specialising in digital transformation, innovation, organisational culture and consumer behaviour. Before his plural existence, he spent more than 13 years in marketing insight and thought leadership roles for an international professional body. He lives by the coast in Cornwall and, when not writing or consulting, is at the beck and call of his soon-to-be-teething daughter.

This book shouldn't exist. However, it does, and, frustratingly, there's a place for it.

The purists among us can still remember (or still cling onto) the true purpose and value of marketing - customer obsession. Also,

- Creating profitable growth
- Bringing market orientation as well as an externalised mindset to strategy and planning
- Applying creativity to commercial choices
- Helping an organisation to decide what not to do
- Building empathy at an institutional level and translating this into loyalty
- Marshalling an organisation's resources to deliver value to its ideal customers in ways that distinguish it from its competitors

That's got nothing to do with AI, 5G, blockchain or bloody millennials (I don't curse the generational cohort, I take aim at the notion 1.8 billion people are the same). This is problem no.1.

Marketing has drifted from customer obsession to a fad. But as interesting as new trends and technologies are, they're not the immediate or absolute answer to your organisation's growth ambitions and competitive challenges. And they're even less likely to lead to productive conversations (or a shred of respect) in the boardroom.

We've forgotten why true marketing is essential and why an organisation will be weakened without it. We've been distracted from the discipline and rigour; marketing offers commercial choices. As the legendary Mark Ritson satirically asked, "What are you doing wasting your time on segmentation, targeting and positioning?"

Compounding this drift to shiny new gizmos is now the tension between marketing and sales. It's akin to that of sibling rivalry, tedious arguing until they've forgotten what started the fight. But, then, it's just something that's become part of their relationship.

Yet, these two functions are closer to the customer and the market than any other in an organisation. Therefore, the functions best placed to make a material impact on growth, profitability and cash flow.

So, why they're often found operating in a disjointed and counter-productive way is a source of much frustration for other executives. And inevitably, behind missed opportunities and competitor delight.

1. The preoccupation with jockeying for influence and control needs to stop
2. The culture of contention and blame between the two functions needs to stop

Mutual respect for both crafts and respective capabilities, and a greater level of understanding, needs to come into play.

In short, marketing and sales teams need to stop sitting in opposition and instead embrace the symbiotic nature of their relationship that the founding fathers of marketing intended. Or at least, a coalition.

So to this book.

Born from these frustrations (and many others), Richard Hadler has been through the labour of love by writing a book.

I've known and worked with Rich for the best part of a decade. His enthusiasm seemingly knows no bounds, and his commercial nous is matched only by his passion for the consumer. He's lived on both sides of the artificial marketing and sales divide, so he speaks from experience, not opinion. And in leading the team at alan. agency, he's immersed in the day-to-day realities facing marketing and commercial leaders.

That's what you'll find in this book. Honesty, pragmatism, and Rich's reassuringly self-confident, glass-half-full outlook (he goes as far to use the term arrogant; I wouldn't).

If you're looking for a compendium of marketing models and theories, send this book back or give it to a colleague or friend in need.

What you will find is one chap's attempt to codify what he's learned – the good, the bad and the freesheet – into practical, useful guidance for others. It's not for everyone, as there's no silver bullet in the growth business. But that's OK; there'll be ideas, takeaways, and guidance that help make a difference for a large proportion of people. Or that simply provide the necessary nudge to think differently about what you're doing in your organisation.

The challenge of growing in an environment of constant change isn't an easy one to solve. But in this book, Rich embraces the challenge.

But if you are looking for a simple answer, it's 'Millennials'. So there you go, no need to read on—millennials (with both hands raised).

THOMAS BROWN

@ThinkStuff

WHAT OTHERS SAY

"The future of B2B marketing has come faster than you thought... and it ain't what it used to be. Now, Data, Customer and Insights-based marketing is the only option for CMOs and their teams – so 'Do or Die'...and take your board and sales teams along your journey with this book."

Philippe Ruttens - Fractional CMO & Revenue Marketeer

———————

"A lot has been written and said on the relationship between sales and marketing. One of the few things everybody can agree on is: alignment is a huge enabler of business growth. Richard's experience on both sides gives him a uniquely informed perspective. Framed with practical, real-world advice rather than theory and jargon, this is one of the books on the subject well worth reading."

Simon Lipscomb - Sales & Marketing Director at Efficio

———————

"Undeniably, Rich is one of the most commercially talented people I will ever have the honour of working for. His relentless enthusiasm for all things sales and marketing is not just a force to be reckoned with but a constant inspiration to all those around him. Marketing: The Bottom Line is one more example of Rich's expertise and practical, no bs approach to encouraging marketing and sales to work with, not against each other."

Tom Andrews - Rev Ops Lead at Permutive

"Rich is a marketing phenomenon. Look at his record. He sells to the world's biggest companies and builds relationships for the long term. We've worked together for a decade, and I've watched Rich train dozens of young professionals to be world class marketers. The book captures everything he knows of the industry. Highly recommended."

Charles Orton-Jones - Freelance Business Journalist

"Today, B2B Marketers need more than ever to clearly understand the sales process and how Sales and Marketing work together. In my experience, Rich and his team consistently hold both sides of this equation up to the mirror. You will understand what I mean if you've worked on both sides. If you haven't had a chance to experience both sides, then this book will help you in your journey."

Kerry Bridge-Collier - Global Marketing Director at Bazaarvoice

---

"I don't know Richard Hadler personally, only of his reputation as an exceptional guy who knows his stuff. Reading this book helped me see how and why he's achieved that reputation. Throughout the pages, he perfectly captures the situation most marketers now find themselves in.

I've spent over 30-years in the world of marketing, working with some of the worlds leading brands, agencies and cultural organisations. That experience has allowed me to experience the type of environment to which Richard urges us to return. I say return because he's right – for many marketers, those days are gone. Marketing decisions are now largely driven by budget, not creativity. As a profession, marketing has, collectively, allowed itself to be pushed to the back of the office and at the bottom of the pecking order. But don't panic; Richard gives workable solutions.

If you buy this book and put it on a shelf unread, as so many of us do with business books, it will be a BIG mistake. Buy it, learn from it – then pass it on to your sales team to read!"

Paul Poole - Founder and Managing Director, Paul Poole (South East Asia) Co., Ltd. - The Sponsorship Experts

INTRODUCTION

The greatest irony in B2B marketing is its inability to understand and effectively represent its own worth to the business it is there to promote. Instead of becoming a celebrated contributor to the bottom line and a strategic influencer of the company direction, marketing has quietly faded into a misunderstood back-office cost centre.

The Oxford Dictionary defines marketing as: The activity of presenting, advertising and selling a company's products or services in the best possible way.

This book addresses the B2B marketing community rather than the B2C space, where many of the topics I cover here are less relevant or more clearly understood already. It examines the disparity between what marketing does (or should do) for the organisations it serves and the recognition it receives for delivering that value. My conclusion might be a hard pill to swallow because I believe the fault lies at, and in truth, deep inside, its own front door. But swallow it you must if you desire a healthy return to the front seat. It is not my intention to offend anyone in the pages that follow. It is an honest assessment from someone who runs a marketing agency but is not actually a marketer. As you read on, I hope you will see why that unique perspective is so critical to identifying both the problem and the solution. I believe my diagnosis is sound and is there for all to see, no matter how hard you scrunch your eyes closed. The solution is equally challenging but ultimately doable.

The good news is that most marketers do have the skillset and intelligence needed to apply the solution. If they are brave enough to try. First, you need to recognise the problem and then do what you do best: design, amplify and present your value in a way that will win you the rewards your ability deserves. But, whether you want to change the company's course, get the respect and recognition you deserve or earn a seat at the board, you must change how you market what you do. There is no other option!

My name is Richard Hadler, and after my introduction to working life in a New Forest holiday park to high-pressure city sales environments and now running a thriving marketing agency, I have seen the best and the worst of sales and marketing. As a hard-nosed, occasionally even condescending salesperson, I wrote this book because marketing has radically changed my mind and opened my eyes to its unrivalled commercial importance. But I can see that, for the most part, it is still undervalued, underutilised and underperforming in the broader business community, and I want to do something to set the story straight. While most business functions continue to advance and evolve, it seems marketing is hiding under a shroud of 'digital everything' and the delusion of shiny new tools when its reality is decades old philosophies and aimless statistics. The world has changed and is not slowing down, but marketing (for the most part) is going backwards and burying its head in the sand.

It's time to awaken the marketing machine and start delivering proper business results (profit).

CONTENTS

PART ONE

Positioning and building bridges.

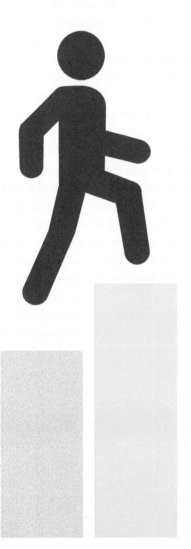

CHAPTER 1

Are we facing the death of B2B marketing?

That is not a clickbait headline – there would be no point as you are already reading my book. It is a genuine question prompted by data, trends, conversations with senior marketers and the reality we all know - even those too afraid to admit it. In truth, I believe the threat of total extinction of our species is unlikely. But to survive, marketing and marketers will have to change, and those who don't adapt will die out soon enough.

The good news is that it is still within our power to decide the future shape of the valuable gift we offer to the world. But we must act now.

This is the choice facing marketers and marketing. We can sit and watch as we drift into an increasingly back-office function, sneered at by salespeople and a begrudged cost centre to the board, or we seize hold of our destiny and lead. It is a choice we have to make, and it is a choice we *can* make if we are brave enough.

This book is about getting marketers to wake up to reality and asking them to do two things. Firstly, recognise what marketing has become and its role in the current landscape and, more importantly, the result of remaining trapped within that subdued stereotype. Secondly, I want them to refocus on the influence they can wield within their organisations. Others may view marketing as rinky-dink or sales support, but they are mistaken. Our problem is that we don't defend our value, which is partly because we don't always recognise it ourselves. I believe that, more than any other business function, marketing can make a difference to the bottom line, dictate boardroom strategies and become famous. We have all the vision, skills, experience and (most importantly of all) access to critical data needed to lead. It is time we seized hold of our value, established a new identity and started showing the world what we can do.

"When you have a commercial mindset and connect the insight and data you have to the business, it shifts the focus you have in marketing," says Iris Meijer, CMO at Verizon Business. *"It's not that we haven't had insight before. We can have all the insight and the data we need, but when you start thinking strategically, it gives you more say in the boardroom because you understand where the company is heading, how you can influence product development and how to work together with sales. Then you don't see yourself anymore as a support function. I see marketing as an enabling function."*

At the time of writing this chapter, less than 5% of CMOs believe they have what it takes to run the company that pays their salary. Only a handful more than that feel they are worthy of occupying a seat in the boardroom. That lack of self-belief and ambition is one of the issues I want to address in this book. I also understand that not every marketing professional has aspirations to run a business. And that is OK – creative marketers with a big picture vision at any level can become formidable forces and change the way marketing is perceived and valued in their companies. Some people simply want to be proud of the work they do each day, sleep well at night knowing they are earning a salary they deserve and hold their head high in the office because others recognise their contribution to the business. That cause is just as worthy. And if that is you, this book is for you too.

Through the chapters that follow, we will start to look at marketing through a different lens. An underlying theme will be the sales versus marketing divide, and I know this topic has been done to death, so I'm not looking to add another voice to the debate – I want to end it! Because I believe the problem, and therefore the solution, is far more profound than solving a 'them and us' inequality. And I also believe I possess a unique view of that scenario because I approach marketing from a salesperson's perspective (cards on the table: a stereotypical, self-confident, brash and bolshy one), who runs a successful marketing agency. Please, don't let my salesperson past put you off. It just means I know what marketers are up against, and I am going to show them how to claim the respect they deserve from their sales team, the board and (perhaps most importantly) themselves.

Bursting the bubble

Confirmation bias is one of the most self-defeating phenomena in any culture, be it national, sector-specific, within a company or in our personal lives. No one likes to listen to people or ideas that annoy them. We all ignore an unwritten list of celebrities who wind us up and cause us to switch channels or huff and puff. When it comes to politics or sport, our opinion on a decision or outcome often arrives long before we hear any details or see the evidence for ourselves. We judge matters by preconditioned bias based on lifelong support, social views or personal preferences, creating echo chambers and spending most of our time surrounded by people with voices like ours, inviting them to reinforce the things we already believe. Over time, this selective influence and internalisation cause messages to get narrower, pre-held beliefs to become stronger, and different groups of people to grow further and further apart. This is not a criticism of anyone, it is simply human nature in action, and we are all prone to influence from the things we like. But it is at the heart of the reason the sales and marketing divide exists and is expanding. As I said, this is no one's fault, but it can be someone's awareness and action that reverses the harmful effects of confirmation bias.

Sales and marketing used to go together like fish and chips, body and soul or safe and sound. But in many companies, it has increasingly become sales and (as an afterthought, if you really must, the cost centre, also known as) marketing. Salespeople have barely noticed their cousins quietly drift away and, as they celebrate their wins with cheers and leaderboards, revel in peer praise and discuss where they will spend their bonuses, their banter reinforces their superior self-belief. As a collective group, the self-talk within sales departments has blindly distanced them from the most valuable relationship they could ever cultivate – with marketing professionals. But it is essential to understand it is not the salespeoples' fault – it is herd culture at work.

Meanwhile, marketers are keeping themselves to themselves, posting blogs, designing logos, talking up creativity, and working to deadlines while waiting to see what their budget dictates they can do next. Their in-house dialogue and corridor conversations draw them deeper into the colouring-in room persona they so vehemently reject before the outside world. And the longer they dwell on the perceived lack of credit, understanding or value afforded to their department, the stronger the reality of those beliefs become. It is time things changed. Like clickbait, the marketing department's reputation has become little more than a clever gimmick everyone else in the business can see right through (even if they too occasionally fall for the quirky one-liner).

Of course, this is not the case in every organisation, but I do see it becoming the norm in too many B2B environments. And in this book, it is the marketers in those places I want to encourage to step up and stake a claim for their rightful level of respect and reward.

When it is executed correctly, I believe marketing becomes the cornerstone of every outstanding business, and marketers can be the architects who give that business its true strength. In the chapters that follow, I want to help marketers smash down the dividing walls, kick open the doors and smash the glass ceiling to show how they can be part of the change that needs to happen. And, as I said at the beginning of this chapter, that change must happen, or the future of marketing, as a function, will have to confront its deathly destiny.

The broad stereotype of a marketing department is not their fault either. In the same way that self-talk has influenced sales departments' attitudes in one direction, marketing has found itself in an ever-decreasing circle. Change is required, and it must start with marketers themselves.

Cracking the code

Salespeople like to talk about the sales funnel, depicting the steps to convert a lead into a signed contract. In fact, the sales funnel is probably the most important model in a salesperson's life. They are, as a breed, fairly singular in their thinking, and to them, getting a sale over the line means everything. And because they are only interested in what comes out of the bottom, they don't often consider the factors that affect or are affected by their sales funnel's activity. How warmed-up leads arrive at the top of a sales funnel as if by magic from a seemingly invisible supply doesn't really matter – as long as they keep coming. (Although the perceived quality of those leads will often be an issue they complain about.) And the work that needs to take place to deliver the goods and services they sell is rarely a concern either; as long as quality is delivered, so they can go back and get repeat orders or ask for referrals. And to be fair to salespeople, they are fulfilling their purpose if they convert leads into sales, and the promises they make to customers result in profitable (this caveat is crucial as we move on to talk bout the bottom line) revenue for the business. It is no wonder the board love successful salespeople – even if that love is tinged with eye-rolling toleration from time to time.

The reality is that a lot of hard work goes into creating the lifeblood supply of leads that feeds a sales funnel. The data from every large organisation on the planet, supported by logic and common sense, should reveal that the quality of leads will always directly influence the sales results. And if leads are the measurable outcome by which a marketing function is measured (if?), we must ensure the rest of the business (not just sales) understands the depth of work, creativity and big picture strategy that goes into that result. At the other end of the sales funnel, successful sales figures can be detrimental to the bigger picture if the strategic objectives are not clearly understood or communicated to the sales team. Selling too much and straining capacity will usually lead to failure to deliver. Trimming margins to undercut the competition is also a recipe for commercial suicide (unless it is part of a short-term strategy, e.g. to win long-term market share). And salespeople who consistently overpromise do no favours to the broader business function and the delivery teams trying to keep up. Scenarios like these are all valid issues to be addressed as after-effects of the sales funnel activities. But in this book, we will concentrate on how marketing directly enhances sales performance (not as a support but as a revenue-generating partner) and how that can dramatically influence the bottom line. We are going to prove that marketing is so much more than a lead-generating function. It may well be dying on its current trajectory, but it can stop the rot, change direction and prove its visionary, creative, analytical genius is the most valuable asset in any organisation.

Alan Turing's famous work, cracking the Enigma code during World War Two, came about through seeing the bigger picture clearly. Yes, he was responsible for taking existing code-breaking equipment to create his Bombe machine, and he developed Turingery, his brilliant technique for breaking unbreakable codes. But it was working out the daily codes that resulted in the real breakthrough. Turning's Hut 8 team realised the code operators would use certain words or phrases each day. Weather reports were standard, so meteorological terms or even the word 'weather' had to appear regularly, and other greetings or salutes were also a given. They also worked out that numbers were spelt rather than using symbols, leading to the creation of the invaluable Eins Catalogue to help speed up the crib process. The work of Alan Turing and his team played a massive part in changing the course of the war, at the very least, speeding up its end by several years. Their achievements saved hundreds of thousands of lives, and it was all down to understanding communication and cracking the code.

After launching a marketing agency under the Raconteur name, we recognised the need for a rebrand and a statement of our identity.

Turing's story inspired us, and the final chapter of this book will explain exactly how we arrived at alan. as our brand. We had created a marketing consultancy business that was making waves and delivering results, but the outside world still saw us as a publishing house. We had to change our language, and that meant cracking the code. The bottom line is that we could have trickled along as the marketing agency division of The Raconteur Group, but we wanted to make a real difference and change the course of marketing.

Marketing professionals have access to data and business intelligence. We are also the masters of language, communication and messaging. And if we can grasp the bigger strategic commercial picture of the business world while making peace with our allies in sales – there will be no stopping us.

CHAPTER 2

The Marketer's Hierarchy of Needs.

Everyone is familiar, even if only by name or from a forgotten module of a degree course, with Maslow's Hierarchy of Needs. It has been a stalwart standard of psychology used to define human motivation for almost eighty years. From sociology to sports and business to behavioural studies, the model has remained relatively unchanged since Abraham Maslow first proposed his idea in the early 1940s. Probably the most significant adaptation is the relationship between the five levels. His original thesis proposed that each level needed to be met independently before reaching the next. Subsequent iterations showed how overlap is possible, and indeed necessary, to achieve true belonging and satisfaction.

In simple terms, Maslow was trying to identify the steps or areas of life every human being (from any culture or age) must fulfil to reach a sense of purpose. And his conclusion suggests that purpose is what makes human endeavour, or simply being alive, both worthwhile and enjoyable. That is perhaps why the model's fundamental principles have lasted so long and why it is still widely applied in every area of life. It is used in the commercial world because people who run large corporations recognised long ago that motivated employees who turn up each day with purpose tend to achieve more. As with the overriding message of this book, everything an employee does must impact the bottom line, in some form or another, or they are not earning their right to that position. And the more an individual or a department can prove their contribution, the more likely they are to feel valued and secure, be creative and wield influence, and have the freedom to realise their potential.

In this chapter, we will adapt Maslow's principle a little and apply it specifically to the modern marketer's role. By doing this, I hope to present a framework you can apply to your current position and use as a roadmap to achieve your ambitions in this worthy profession of marketing.

But before we do that, and just in case you are among the one-in-ten who are unfamiliar with Maslow's original work, let me share a 3-minute recap of the original theory. (If you can quote Maslow in your sleep, please feel free to skip down to the marketer's version.)

Maslow's Hierarchy of Needs

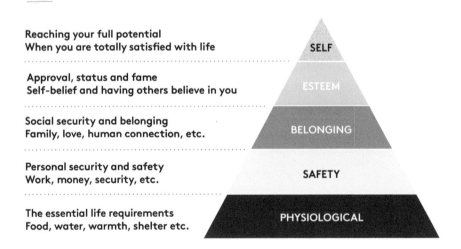

Reaching your full potential
When you are totally satisfied with life — **SELF**

Approval, status and fame
Self-belief and having others believe in you — **ESTEEM**

Social security and belonging
Family, love, human connection, etc. — **BELONGING**

Personal security and safety
Work, money, security, etc. — **SAFETY**

The essential life requirements
Food, water, warmth, shelter etc. — **PHYSIOLOGICAL**

PHYSIOLOGICAL NEEDS. This refers to a person's essential, primal nature – or what we all need to keep our physical bodies healthy and operationally sound. These needs include things like air to breathe, clothes to wear, food, water, warmth and general wellness. This need becomes the foundation level of the model, setting down the understanding that a person who lacks these essential life requirements will look to secure them before addressing higher goals.

SAFETY NEEDS. Having established a reasonable level of immediate physical comfort, an individual will look to secure personal safety. They will seek to establish financial stability through work or investment, the ability to protect themselves from external threats and strive to achieve a sense of being in control of their surroundings.

BELONGING NEEDS. The third level of human need is the desire to belong. We are, by nature, social animals, and for most people, family is the single greatest drive in their lives. Likewise, in our social circles, working environments and home life, we are happiest when we feel like we belong to the group. Love comes in many shapes and forms, but a lack of human connection and feeling loved is a recipe for unhappiness. Among the many things we all learned during the COVID-19 pandemic, one is that: social interaction is a basic human need.

I want to offer a non-judgemental but potentially controversial personal observation at this point. There are still two steps to go in Maslow's model, but I think too many people, today, settle for mediocrity in their lives by taking the easy option of stopping here. For the majority of people, being fed and watered while feeling safe and loved is enough. I'll come back to this point when we get into the marketer's version of the model.

ESTEEM NEEDS. After achieving a sense of belonging and being loved comes the need to feel respected within the communities where we spend our time. This typically manifests itself in two ways. Firstly, we seek approval from those around us through status, fame, or simply being recognised, liked, or afforded others' attention. Secondly (and, according to Maslow, a higher type of esteem) is the sense of self-respect and the core inner belief that you are becoming the best version of yourself.

SELF ACTUALISATION NEEDS. The highest level of need or achievement in the hierarchy is the state where a person can reach their potential. When all other physical, material, emotional and social needs are satisfied, the complete individual, full of confidence and self-esteem, can go out and pursue whatever they choose in life. The sky really is the limit for someone at the peak of Maslow's Hierarchy of Needs.

Why do we need a marketer's hierarchy of needs?

When I was pulling together ideas for this book, I wanted to find a way of demonstrating it is worth the risk to challenge the status quo. My experience in the high stakes, cutthroat world of sales showed me that a poor salesperson has a short lifecycle (sometimes drastically short), and even an average one needs to be continually pushing the needle to survive. Marketing is a more passively dangerous environment to make a living. As a marketer, it has become possible to reach a level of mediocrity and establish a comfortable career there. In reference to my earlier note about people being happy to stay at Maslow's triangle's 'belonging' level, I would suggest many marketers have settled into this position and are probably blissfully unaware of their circumstances. The problem is that the current commercial environment puts their positions increasingly under threat and well and truly in the endangered business species category. I absolutely realise this is a generalisation. There will be many reading this who are still flying the flag for great marketing and making waves in their companies and industries. I have the privilege of knowing some truly inspirational marketers, and their example has inspired many elements of this book.

As I researched the history of marketing and the way elements of marketing have shifted from big picture creativity toward more sedentary, task-driven activities, it reminded me of The Sorites Paradox (or the paradox of the heap). This describes the unanswerable question of defining the moment a heap of sand with one million grains stops being recognised as a 'heap' if you were to remove one grain at a time. It appears to me that the ability to make a substantial material difference to the bottom line of a business has been removed from marketing's power (one grain at a time) in recent decades, and I fear that very few people have noticed.

That is why I created the Marketer's Hierarchy of Needs. Because if marketers can see where they are on this model, they can make clear decisions about their future survival or preferably choose to help put marketing where it should be – seizing back control and spearheading the revolution. So here is how it works.

The Marketer's Hierarchy of Needs

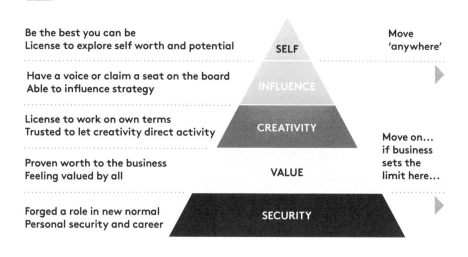

SECURITY NEEDS. While security might be a closer match to the second level in the original pyramid of needs, there is no doubt that the primary focus of having a job is, first and foremost, holding onto the position. So, the first area I would encourage any marketer to examine is whether their current role is secure. In the light of an ever-changing, (almost) post-pandemic, increasingly flexible and automated world, is the current shape of marketing valued and sustainable as a profitable business function? Here is a highly personalised take on the question if you are reading this book as a person who works in marketing. If your company had to start making cut-backs next week and twenty per cent of the entire workforce was under threat, how would you rate your chances of keeping your role? You could look at other departments and suggest they might be the first to go, and you could argue the toss over who provides the most value, but the reality is: the decision-makers are unlikely to share your view. And, while marketing departments probably contribute more to the bottom line than their employers appreciate, the irony is that most have failed to demonstrate their worth (or market themselves) to the board.

VALUE NEEDS. If a marketer's role is secure (even after a twenty per cent reduction in the workforce), it means the board or business owners believe marketing has value. So here is my next question. Do the decision-makers in the business believe marketing is important because their MBA and every book or training course on the subject tell them it is? Or because they recognise the contribution of the marketing people they employ? In other words, is the marketer, or marketing division, genuinely valued within the business? I believe this is vitally important because if all someone wants is a well-paid job in a city, there are probably better options, and certainly ones with more long-term security prospects than marketing. If you are serious about marketing as a career and desire to be the best you can be within that role, the minimum requirement is to feel valued by those who pay your salary. Being valued should be a given for every employee, for sure, but you cannot take this for granted, and I encourage you to find out what the people leading your business really think. If you do not get a satisfactory answer, I would ask you to consider a strategy to change their mind or a plan to change your employer.

CREATIVITY NEEDS. There is a big difference between being valued and being trusted. A rugby coach might value various squad members and pick them for the team, but he will only give the captain's armband to the one he trusts. If you enjoy entertaining guests at home, you might try out new recipes on a few close friends, but for the big occasion when you are out to impress, you will always return to your tried and tested signature dish. And while you might ask Google what your symptoms are telling you, when your child's temperature reaches forty-one, and the blotches are getting worse – you will call a doctor. So, my question to marketers is: does the business that employs you to do marketing trust you to do marketing? You see, part of the problem I want to address in this book is the shackles that a modern definition of marketing has put on creativity. Instead of being free to design innovative, original campaigns and big ideas, marketing is becoming a succession of tick-box activities: blogs, media posts, editorials, adverts, AdWords, reports and meaningless research.

MOVE ON. Maslow didn't offer the option to change the narrative; he just pointed out what was needed to move up the pyramid to the next level. In my Marketer's Needs model, you will notice an arrow between the Value and Creativity sections. That is there because I believe you have a choice. If you truly want to make a difference, become famous in your world, or simply be the best marketer you can be, you can only do that if the people who pay you believe in you. Being valued is a great start. But being allowed to show what you can do is the new marketing standard in the new normal – whatever shape that might turn out to be. So I have called this arrow 'move on' because the hard truth is that a business that doesn't trust its marketing department to get creative will never let that department influence strategic policy and create magic. I'm not suggesting you make impulse decisions with your career here – simply that you think about what you need as a person, and you give the business a reasonable time to prove it can deliver on that need. If it can't, and you are as good as you think you are, there is no doubt there will be a company out there that speaks your language.

INFLUENCE NEEDS. Despite my earlier tongue-in-cheek slur on people who settle for belonging, I accept entirely (and genuinely do respect) any marketer who is happy to be a trusted creative in their role. Not everyone can or even needs to have their sights set on a seat at the board (there wouldn't be enough positions to go around for a start). However, if you can crack the 'creativity delivers value' code and demonstrate that marketing has access to critical market data and knowledge of how to wield it, you can become a powerful influence. For me, this is the pinnacle of where marketing should be in the future evolution of business. No other function has such a comprehensive understanding of customers, buying habits, relationships, future trends, and the products and services the market actually wants. All we are missing, and I accept I am generalising, some marketers are hot on this already, is expert financial business acumen. And that is another issue I will address later in this book.

SELF NEEDS. I have already stated that being influential is the pinnacle for marketing. So, why have I included the fifth tier in my pyramid? The honest answer is because I wanted to mirror Maslow as closely as possible, and he had five levels in his model. But there is a direct link between being a person of authority and influence in any organisation and achieving self-actualisation. You see, once you are in demand and your value is fully recognised, you can pretty much do whatever you want in your career. Being a famous marketer with a portfolio of memorable campaigns, stunning big ideas, and market-changing moments to your name opens doors and creates unlimited opportunities. Where do you want marketing to take you?

The Marketer's Hierarchy of Needs is a *kind of* framework for the rest of this book, and I will refer back to it as we explore the solutions and stories that will forge a way to the top. In the next chapter, we travel back to the beginning to discover where it all started and why it seems nobody cares about marketing anymore. First, I want you to examine your current situation and ask where you are on the pyramid. I suspect there will be CMOs and perhaps even CROs who are confidently living in the Influence or Self levels. Other experienced marketers (without the leadership title) might also knowingly nod as they read these pages and be assured that they and others appreciate their worth. If that is you, please share this book with someone who needs it more than you do (when you have finished reading!).

If you are on the bottom two rows, or you feel you have not even achieved the feeling of Value, I hope the rest of this book leaves you fully equipped for the fight ahead. Because it will be a fight, but it is one you can win, and I aim to give you the confidence, education and practical skills you need to progress your own hierarchy pyramid as you read on.

Taking practical steps towards the bottom line

Use the questions and criteria in this practical section to identify your current position on the Marketer's Hierarchy of Needs model. Then decide where you would like to go with your career and start to think about the steps you can take to get there. (We will return to this model and your progress later in the book.)

Your hierarchy of needs as a marketer

1. .... **SELF**
2. ....

1. .... **INFLUENCE**
2. ....

1. .... **CREATIVITY**
2. ....

1. .... **VALUE**
2. ....

1. .... **SECURITY**
2. ....

1. Where do you think you are now?
2. What needs to happen to move up a level?

Notes:

....

....

....

....

....

....

....

....

....

....

....

....

....

Do you have SECURITY in your role? Do you believe you have clarity about these things within your role?

- Do you have a defined role and clear responsibilities and do you know what is expected of you? □
- Key Performance Indicators that allow you and your managers to measure if your deliver a result. □

Success at this level should begin to create a sense of security that your role is secure.

Write a few lines to describe what needs to happen for you to fulfil this criteria and move to the next level:

....

....

....

....

....

....

....

....

....

....

....

....

Are you VALUED within the team? Can you recognise and demonstrate the value you bring to your role?

- Do you see how you fit within the broader marketing team? Whose work does your work influence? ☐
- Learn where your output benefits results. Identify the part you play in the bigger picture. ☐
- Decide if others recognise your contribution. How can you make sure your efforts are seen? ☐

In a perfect world, we would all like to think others see us for the value we bring. But we do not live in a perfect world, so take a leaf from the salesperson's playbook and find ways to make your results shine.

Write a few lines to describe what needs to happen for you to fulfil this criteria and move to the next level:

....

....

....

....

....

....

....

....

....

Can you work CREATIVELY off-piste? Is your voice heard and respected within the team?

- Are all your tasks tick-box exercises, or are you afforded the freedom to experiment? ☐
- Can you begin to define your own role - where the result is more important than the means? ☐
- Do your peers ask your opinion, and are you part of the broader marketing conversation? ☐

When you are asked your opinion and get involved in the broader conversation around the direction of the marketing team's efforts, you can call yourself a true marketer.

Write a few lines to describe what needs to happen for you to fulfil this criteria and move to the next level:

....

....

....

....

....

....

....

....

....

....

Does your INFLUENCE reach beyond marketing? Does your work and your voice get noticed beyond marketing?

- Can you converse with your sales team with commercial parity? Or do you feel they look down on you? ☐
- Can you converse with the board or other heads of departments with commercial parity? ☐
- Can you describe your department's contribution to the business with 100% confidence and pride? ☐

This book is about putting marketers in a place where they can drive the business forward from the inside. To do that you need to be in the driving seat and that means stepping outside of the marketing department and having bigger conversations with other Senior business stakeholders.

Write a few lines to describe what needs to happen for you to fulfil this criteria and move to the next level:

....

....

....

....

....

....

....

....

....

Where do you want to go as a marketer? Are you happy and fulfilled in what you are doing?

- Could you do more with your position? Could you use your influence to push the business further forward? ☐
- Where else could you take the business or your career as a marketer or entrepreneur? ☐

My ambition is for this model, and the rest of the content in this book, to encourage and guide marketers to the strategic forefront of their organisations and drive their careers and opportunities to new heights.

Write a few lines to describe what needs to happen for you to fulfil this criteria and move to the next level:

....

....

....

....

....

....

....

....

....

....

....

CHAPTER 3

Nobody cares about marketing anymore. Do you want the cure?

Do you ever feel like nobody cares about you until something goes wrong? Does it seem like marketing is the first in line for cutbacks and backhanded insults but last on the list for a rise or a pat on the back when record sales months arrive? Please forgive me (I'll make my full apology in chapter six), but I have been among the guilty here. I have laughed along as my fellow salespeople blamed the colouring-in department for sending them rinky-dink leads or completely missing the point. I've also sat in boardrooms, discussing what the marketing department should be doing when no marketing representative was present to offer an inside or informed opinion. How does that make you feel?

You could be forgiven for feeling unappreciated if that is how things work in your organisation. But seriously. Are you looking for forgiveness, or do you want a chance to shape the entire future of marketing? When I was a salesperson (and again, please remember there is a full apology coming), I swear there have been times I've walked into the marketing department and sensed people cower at my presence. If you are looking for sympathy, understanding or forgiveness for not being appreciated, you are reading the wrong book. I want to help you find your feet, recognise your own worth and promote yourself into the positions you deserve. I have learned that great marketers are worth their weight in bottom-line profit, and I believe they can become the cornerstone of every organisation's success. Yes, I have been a salesperson and developed a shortsighted view of marketing's value, but now I see things from the other side and understand how hard it can be to prove your value. I sympathise with the modern marketer's position and am happy to apologise for my past misconceptions, but I want to do much more. I want to create a platform for marketing to recapture its voice.

I spend a lot of my time speaking to marketers who have a 'how did I get here?' approach to their career. They followed a well-trodden path, showing creative tendencies at school and college, achieving a degree in digital marketing, economics, graphic design, media studies etc., at university, then launching their career. Several interviews and years later, they find themselves in a comfy B2B marketing role as part of a creative team, looking busy and barely noticed by anyone else.

Other marketers I know have fire in their bellies and frustration running through their veins at the injustice of the status quo. They planned their path into marketing and had visions of their name in lights, celebrated as the one whose creative spark changed the game. Maybe you identify with either of these profiles, but most likely, you live somewhere in between. To be blunt, I don't care what your aspirations were two, three or five years ago. The door that led you into marketing has slammed shut, and what you have done ever since offers little value in today's commercial landscape. Regardless of how you got here...you need to start again.

Whether you studied marketing or you fell into this career, you need to reinvent yourself. It is not just newspaper and magazine ads that are history; everything about marketing has changed. If you are sitting behind a marketer's desk because that is where the tide of your career led you, your only chance to avoid drowning is educating yourself on all things business. And by that, I mean commercial, financial, process, sales and marketing. If making your mark in marketing was always the goal, I want to challenge you that you 'no longer know what you need to know'. The world has changed again and is showing no signs of stopping.

This book is not going to teach you anything about how to 'do' marketing. I am not as qualified as others to deliver that sort of content. And the exact point I want to make is that anything I could teach would be out of date before we went to print anyway. Yes, most of marketing's fundamental principles are pretty much constant, but how to apply them is changing faster than I can type this sentence.

Instead, the book's purpose is to make you a marketer who can turn their position into a career, influence the direction of their organisation, stand shoulder to shoulder with sales leaders and board members, own your space in the business, and make yourself famous. But, if you want to learn anything from this book or the world around you, you have to start by admitting to yourself what I believe you already know. You have to see that marketing faces a life-limiting prognosis, and it will only deteriorate unless it is treated professionally and urgently.

This is the challenge

Today, most organisations view marketing as a cost centre instead of a valuable strategic asset that generates a profitable return directly to the bottom line. Marketers who have a similar view of themselves and carry on doing their job description (churning out graphics, blog posts, updates, sign-ups and other collateral) as requested must be aware – doing this puts them in grave danger of sleep-walking into unemployment. Because when things get tight around the bottom line, which parts of the business do you think are most at risk of the cut?

Cutting people's jobs is not a flippant statement or idea. I am writing this book in the second half of 2021 as the UK is hopefully starting its recovery from the COVID-19 pandemic. And the fact is: one in ten marketers lost their jobs during that period. Other professions would have suffered too, but profit and recognition of strategic value will have played a significant role in deciding which roles went first. And the same thing could happen again.

The solution is becoming a business-first marketer. That is the only way to unleash your creativity and release yourself from the bonds of back-office obscurity and budget restrictions. I realise those two sentences sound like a contradiction, but it refers to a process, and the contents of this book describe what connects the two ideas. As soon as you can prove yourself to the business as a profit-generating asset, fluent in the boardroom's language and valuable in your sales team's eyes, you can write your own agenda and release your creative flair. I'm not going to lie here; this will not be easy, but please bear with me because it *is* possible.

When Tom Hanks walks out onto a film set and makes a creative request, suggests a change in the script or asks for an expensive scene to be reshot, what do you think happens? People bow to his influence because they respect his experience – yes. But, full disclosure here, the main reason is the impact his presence has on the movie's performance at the box office. If Lady GaGa decides half the orchestra her management team have hired are not up to the performance she demands, do you think they will worry about overspending on the budget to find a replacement? When the creative director is also the star of the show, they make the money decisions. If Lionel Messi's contract says he must start in every match he is deemed fit enough to play in, does that stop the club owners from signing that contract? And if he tells his manager he doesn't like the role he has been asked to play, who wins the argument? Goals speak volumes because they add value to the bottom line of any organisation.

Business is no different from showbiz or sport in this respect. When an influencer or decision-maker's contribution to the overall business goals (i.e. revenue and profit) are recognised and valued, their voice amplifies, and their opinions start to count. This is a three-step process, and I am going to describe that to you now:

STEP ONE. Become a business-savvy marketer.

I have mentioned bottom-line profit several times in the build-up to this point, but that might not always be the goal. It is your responsibility to find out the size and shape of your organisation's top-line strategic goals. For most, I would suggest profitability is the central pivot. But if the owners are looking to sell, they might focus on turnover; or if growth by acquisition is their aim, increased brand awareness could be the strategic direction. You might even work for a not-for-profit organisation built on external funding and investment for a future acquisition, innovation or charitable cause. Whatever the board's strategic goal, you need to know why you are doing your thing in marketing. Understand what you are looking to achieve for the wider business and measure everything against its contribution to that objective.

More than that, though, you need to show the world you under-stand these things. You know how we encourage children not to worry about what other people think and emphasise that it's 'more important to be yourself'? It might be a good principle on one level, I get that, but in business, it is nonsense. In the real world, you cannot afford always to be an idealist. Just being great is not enough. One of the lessons from the salespersons' playbook that I want to share with you in a later chapter is the value of self-promotion. Ironically, the mantra, 'a poor product, wellmarketed will always outsell a great product, poorly marketed' is a perfect example of my point. Does anybody really believe the most famous hamburger in the world is the best, or a certain fizzy, caffeine-based drink is going to make your life better? Was VHS better than Betamax, CDs more versatile than MiniDiscs or FaceBook a safer and happier place than FriendsReunited? If you want to become a professional marketer, you need to understand the commercial business you are working for and make sure the powers-that-be know that you know.

STEP TWO. Be more creative and don't hold back.

Too many marketing departments become budget-driven functions hidden within the mechanics of a department. The board decides they need a logo, content for the website, advertising campaigns, banners, market research, congruent styles, social media management, etc. Based on last year's budget and the broader performance of the company, they then decide this year's budget and send the number to the department head. The team leaders then gather around and reverse engineer a plan around that budget: choosing how much and how many marketing activities they can afford to pursue.

What happened to the big idea? You can't explore space by breaking down the component parts of a car or unlock the secrets of quantum physics with a Bunsen Burner and the contents of a school science cupboard. Even with access to an entire scrapyard or twenty classrooms, you would fail. Marketing success is not determined by the budget, the amount of work you do or even how well you do it. You need to start with a big idea. Instead of reacting to a budget, proactively create solutions for your business. The best marketers in the world today are those whose creativity is allowed the freedom to think. Later in the book, I have included some of the exercises and techniques we use to teach our clients and help rekindle their good old fashioned creativity and marketing flair.

'That is all well and good, Rich', I hear you thinking. 'We are the undervalued back-office function, the colouring-in department you mentioned at the beginning of this chapter – no one is going to allow us to work like that!' I totally get it and understand why you might react like that now. But I want to show you how to change the landscape, take charge of the higher ground and push the needle. And the change begins when marketers start to take on the mantle of business-savvy professionals. I promise you, when you learn to speak the board's language and win their respect by proving your knowledge, they will listen to your reasoning.

In chapter twelve, I will come back to the idea that you should: be as good as you think you are.

STEP THREE. Cut back the shrinking violet and let your colours bloom.

Stop letting the world happen to you. Interrogate your intelligence, challenge the status quo, stand up for your creativity and take control of your future. No one is going to do it for you – the world isn't that kind. But if you make an effort to get beneath the surface of marketing and business wisdom, you can carve a course that will be both satisfying and rewarding. I know it is possible because, in the same way I speak to many lost marketers, I also rub shoulders with those who dictate corporate strategy at the highest level.

A few years back, I started waking up feeling like I had barely been to sleep. Instead of being the life and soul of the office (even on a Monday morning) and geeing everyone else into top gear, I would creep in at lunchtime. To start with, I thought it was an underlying flu bug that would eventually sort itself out. I tried various concoctions of vitamin C, D and B supplements, but with little effect, and things just got worse. My muscles ached constantly, I felt sick, lethargy took over my body, and the simplest tasks left me ridiculously fatigued. After weeks of 40% performance (and dropping), I eventually ended at the doctor's door. I hate doctors.

One consultation followed another, and no one could diagnose the problem, leaving me to suffer far too many days of self-pity before they finally worked out what was going on. I had (in fact, I still have) an underactive thyroid. Now, I take one levothyroxine tablet every morning, and my bounce is back. It is incredible how one 12mm mixture of chemicals can kickstart my thyroid into action and set my entire body into top form. It is only writing this that I realise how much I take that tablet for granted now – and I never forget to take it.

So, I want to propose a challenge to you today. Ask yourself how much of this chapter rings true for you. Can you see how the rules are changing around you, and without your permission? As I mentioned in the introduction, I am a salesperson who runs a successful marketing agency. I don't say it is successful as a boast (although I am proud of what we have achieved), but to prove I know what I am talking about. I believe my diagnosis of marketing's current condition is correct, and I want to prescribe the cure.

Every morning, take one BCB Pill to improve Business; Creativity; and Backbone. Make sure that each day you sit down at your desk, you improve in each of these areas of your professional life. One incremental change per day will soon add up, and before you know it, you will be making waves because you will be full of BCB...

BUSINESS. (Become a business-savvy professional marketer.) Educate yourself each day about business: both the commercial aspects of the numbers and specific aspects of the business sector where you work. Learn to market your value to the critical internal customers you serve. Know your audience (the board) and learn to articulate the business in a language they understand. (We will cover this in more detail in the second half of the book.)

CREATIVITY. (Be more creative and don't hold back.) Approach each new project with the big idea first. Stop thinking in terms of platforms, impressions, views and reporting metrics. Imagine the final destination (in line with the business goal) and create an idea that will take you there. (I'll come back to this later in the book, but here is a hint: today's marketing tactics won't make you famous.)

BACKBONE. (Cut back the shrinking violet and let your colours bloom.) Wake up to the reality of the situation. Modern marketing is dying, and getting in tune with the future is the only way to survive. That takes bravery, self-belief and determination. But guts alone will not get you there; you need to prove your worth through results, maturity and leadership. In this book, I want to show you how – are you willing to try?

We will visit each of these topics in more detail later, starting with the following four chapters; opening up Pandora's Box (in a controlled environment, of course), we begin to tackle the sales-marketing divide.

CHAPTER 4

Two sides of
the same coin.

If you are still reading, I am assuming you have got over the first hurdle. You have owned up to the stark reality: marketing has a problem that needs solving. Good!

As with all life's challenges, awareness is half of the battle (and we are only in chapter four), so we are on the right track. Chapter eight will address the second challenge facing today's marketing professionals: how to forge a place of parity alongside your sales compatriots. Before we work out how to close that ever-widening divide, I want to dive deeper into its murky mysteries and examine why it exists.

Sales and marketing rolls off the tongue, and so it should. Think about it. The ultimate goals are absolutely and unequivocally the same – to generate 'profitable' sales for the business. So, why does a 'them and us' mentality prevail in almost every organisation in the world? You cannot have strong walls without deep foundations; the most talented attacking line-up will fail to win the game if the defence leaks goals, and it doesn't matter how many Michelin Stars you have if your ingredients are shoddy. Sales and marketing are two sides of the same coin, and seeing each other as rivals or even bearing the slightest grudge will not help anybody's cause.

The truth is (and this is Richard, the salesperson talking), the cause of the problem usually lies inside the sales office door. Salespeople do have an air of arrogance and superiority. They are self-confident, they know-it-all, and they can be condescending at times – absolutely. Most of them tend to completely misunderstand what marketing is even all about (some are a bit more switched on than others). Ask most salespeople to define the role of marketing, and they will say something like, 'to generate leads'. In addition to this reply, they will even think, or add out loud, 'and most of the leads they generate are rubbish'. I can imagine marketers everywhere nodding in agreement lamenting 'bloody sales' even as I write this. Well, it is true.

There are two essential things for marketers to understand from this reality. Firstly, if you have salespeople in your business who fit the stereotype description above, you should be grateful that these hungry, go-getter, deal-closing professionals are on your team. Secondly, you should realise that they are unlikely to change their view of you on their own. If you want them to appreciate you and see you as a benefit to their efforts (maybe even to view you as equal partners in the team), you need to change. They absolutely should value you and recognise your contribution. But they are not going to do that just because you wave a colourful brochure in their face. Like Blackadder once said to Baldrick, 'I trust him about as much as I would trust an anteater not to eat ants'. You cannot expect salespeople to think about anything other than selling. And to be frank, why would you want them to?

But it *is* possible to prove you understand their needs, demonstrate how your work helps them close more deals and show them why they could barely breathe without you. It is simply a case of giving the salespeople in your team a different lens and letting them see from the other side of the coin. You are an expert marketer, after all. Sharing messages by telling stories is what you do – so this should come easily to you.

Look, I understand that what I am presenting here is not a new idea. This conversation has raged for years, and it would be a fair point to ask why my argument is any different. Well, it seems that even for all the content out there telling marketers to step up, they don't. And what I am suggesting is that as vigorously as you agreed with my 'bloody sales' comment just now, you take the threat of not acting seriously this time.

Two sides of the story

In 2017, I attended a rinky-dink content marketing seminar somewhere in the middle of Somerset. It was one of those events that seemed like a good idea at the time, but when the day arrives, you can think of a hundred better things to do. I can't even remember the name of the venue or event. As expected, most of the talks were drab and uninspiring – the same tired old digital marketing how-to and content themed theory. One session did leave an impression, although it was an extension of the idea that emerged in my mind. In fact, it may well be the style of the person presenting the session who caused me to pay any attention at all.

He looked like a nutty professor, strolling up and down in his white coat and thick-rimmed glasses, muttering to himself between sentences and stopping every two or three steps to tug at his bottom lip. It was his style that intrigued me as much as anything, and he certainly stood out from other stereotypes I'd seen that day. He was sharing his ideas on the six essential aspects of storytelling in B2B marketing. And as I looked around the half-empty room, I saw that everyone else seemed more interested in him than his subject too.

This is what he shared:

1. Immerse your audience in the story. This means engaging their senses and emotions so they feel like they are involved in the story themselves – not just listening to it.

2. Tell a personal story. Make the story about a person or a problem they can identify with – making the audience feel like this could be them.
3. Take them on a journey. Your stories should be moving in more ways than one – meaning they should take the listener from one place (or opinion) to another place (or opportunity).
4. Make your characters seem real. Stories do not need to be true to contain powerful truths, but they do need to make sense to real people – so tell truthful stories.
5. Show. Don't tell. The old story of giving a man a fish or showing him how to fish is still relevant today – and is evidence of the power of showing over telling.
6. End with a positive takeaway. People can listen for an hour but will only remember a few minutes of content – so make sure they leave with the soundbite of your choice.

As this pacing professor of storytelling was waxing lyrical in the build-up to his positive takeaway, my mind had wandered elsewhere. I enjoyed his performance and agreed with his well-made points, but I heard a different story – I was listening as a salesperson. It suddenly hit me that each of these guidelines for marketers has a mirror-image rule for sales. Marketers create stories – salespeople tell stories. And there is a difference.

Now, look at the salespersons' version of the same six aspects of storytelling:

1. *Immerse your audience into why your product exists.* This expands the story idea (brand) into why you have developed it into a product or solution – exploring the need it fulfils and getting involved in the story. If you don't know something intimately, how can you sell it?
2. *Tell a story about how your product helps.* Introduce your audience to someone like them, who used your product to solve their problems – and exactly how this happened.
3. *Take them on a journey from their problem to your product.* Address your audience's current situation and move them towards your

product – this is the real heart (or art) of sales storytelling. True sales skill is so much more than simply translating features into benefits – it is becoming the storyteller and feeling the need.

4. *Make your solution seem real and affordable.* Demonstrate that choosing to use your product is the easiest, most realistic and obvious next step in the world – we call this pre-empting objections.

5. *Case studies and use cases.* Nothing seals a sales deal as effectively as a hands-on demonstration or a real-life example from a third-party voice your audience recognises and trusts. People need to know the message is tangible and real, or they will not buy anything.

6. *End with the best reason for them to buy.* I always feel like the best sales presentations (stories) close themselves. But as any good salesperson will tell you – if you don't ask, you won't get a result.

You may or may not learn something from the two versions of the storytelling steps narrative described above. I imagine there was nothing new there for many readers. But I hope you noticed my main point. The two lists mirror the same story – only the application of the steps has changed. Likewise, sales and marketing as functions leading to profitable revenue for the business are part of the same endeavour. They should be two sides to the same golden coin.

If you want to achieve an equal-partnership (share the work, effort and rewards) relationship with your sales team, how about this for a positive takeaway: tell the *same* story.

Marketing guru Seth Godin wrote a brilliant book on storytelling in marketing: All Marketers Are Liars. Interestingly, a later reprint of the book included a note suggesting that putting 'liars' in the title was a mistake. Godin referenced this to one of its central themes; how a good story must be authentic. Truth always hits the spot with a listener, even if the story is clearly a fable, anecdote or example. There never was a race between a tortoise and hare...

Over the book's 220 pages, he explains why our brains are hard-wired to listen to stories. If a brand, or a big idea, can find a distinctive (and true) story that connects with its target customer's heart and soul, the results can be transformative. You only have to look at the brands on everyone's lips to see this truth in big, bright, bold letters displayed all around the world. Every marketing professional knows this truth as it is the pinnacle of what they would love to achieve. Salespeople know it too – but they don't really care why it works.

That is why another of Godin's rules is so critical to my point in this chapter. Because the story you tell also has to be consistent. Like detectives on a crime scene who look for inconsistencies in the witness statements and those tantalising missing clues that just don't add up, customers will detect incongruence. They may not notice the exact gap in the message, the written and verbal variances, or think it odd that a salesperson hasn't even seen your advert. But the discrepancies will register as contradictions somewhere in their psyche, which might just set off the 'big fat lie' alarm. That's where the poor (or in many cases non-existent) communication between sales and marketing can become a stumbling block to success. I'm not just talking about lost sales here. Most people can forgive mistakes, but lies cut far deeper and can kill relationships for life.

And guess what? Salespeople will always blame marketing in these scenarios because they interpret this as poor-quality leads. And while that is clearly not the case, only marketers can do something about it. Marketers are the true creators and originators of these stories. It is up to you to make sure your sales team are singing the same tune. 'Yes, Rich, that is all well and good', I can hear you saying again, 'but how do I get their attention and how do I make them understand?'

Trust me, here, we are moving towards the unification plan. First, I need you to understand a little more about the inside of your sales counterparts' hearts and minds. The more you know about their motivations, the easier it will be to invite them into the story of your future successes as a team. So, in the next chapter, I will share the start of my story and how I became a hard-nosed, slightly arrogant, certainly opinionated salesperson; then, we will begin to uncover the salesperson's psyche and discover what makes them tick. Until then, let me leave you with a bit of a clue.

Keep it simple and keep it moving

Working towards the same goal is not just about 'piquing interest' by marketing and 'closing' by sales; it's about moving your potential customers through a joined-up journey. I like to call this 'telling a consistent story'. The maximum danger of a disconnect (where most opportunities are lost) is at lead handover. If the story shifts here, customer trust goes up in smoke. Creating a clear and concise storytelling framework that all parties agree to will make the telling as natural as turning a page. Remember how we talked about being creative and coming up with the big idea first in the last chapter? The same principle applies to your stories. The headline idea doesn't need to be an entire novel – it just needs to make an impact.

Legend has it that the great Ernest Hemingway would bet people ten dollars he could move them, or make them cry, with a six-word story. He won his bet almost every time with the following tragic tale... For sale, baby shoes, never worn.

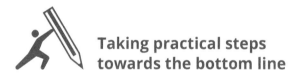 **Taking practical steps towards the bottom line**

Write a story for your brand, following the six-step structure detailed in this chapter. Then transform that story into a salesperson's version, to try and understand the subtleties of the different approaches. This will form part of your battle plan when you converse customers and sales team, and will demonstrate just how deeply you understand your brand's power.

MARKETING VERSION	SALES VERSION
1)	1)
2)	2)
3)	3)
4)	4)
5)	5)
6)	6)

CHAPTER 5

Do you want
sauce with that?

Growing up in the picturesque, olde-worlde micro-culture of the New Forest tends to squash business ambition and age people faster than their years. Most of the people I knew as a kid are still going with the flow of forest life. And if I'd forgotten my trusty sauce bottle the day Iain sat down for his scampi and chips, I might still be there listening to the birds singing in the trees and charming holidaymakers with an array of quips and tricks. But then again, I've noticed how lucky breaks always catch up with enthusiasm and persistence in the end, so maybe it was only a matter of time before I found my way to the big city.

I was 16 years old, doing my A-Levels and working every available hour at Sandy Balls Holiday Village, serving tables and behind the bar. I loved the idea of earning my own money and, always looking for ways to raise a smile or a reaction, I developed a few tricks to keep customers in good spirits or a tipping mood. One of my favourites was to hide a tomato ketchup bottle behind my back as I placed the guest's food on the table. I had observed that 95% of the time, especially with families, if I asked the question, "Any sauce with that?" they would reply "ketchup". And I soon perfected the art of placing the bottle on the table in synchrony with the '...up'. I made a lot of days (and piggybank filler) that way.

One day a solo-diner in the restaurant simply stared at me quizzically as the sauce bottle landed in unison with his tomatoey request. It was almost as if he had just had an epiphany, and I too froze in his moment, waiting for him to say something or start eating, before moving off with a silent teenage 'OK then' rolling through my mind. I soon forgot about the incident and returned to the buzz and busyness of holiday park life. It all came rushing back two weeks later, accompanied by an embarrassing glow, as all the staff (350 in total and me 349th from the top) were called into a meeting and introduced to the new Managing Director.

Iain, the man I had shared a long and surreal moment with a few weeks earlier, was introduced as the new boss and stood up to give his maiden speech. He promised to make Sandy Balls great, spoke about his ideas for the park, and announced a few changes and new appointments. To finish, he asked if the young lad who had served him scampi and chips a few weeks earlier would join him on stage and, as I jostled my way through the company ranks to join him, he proceeded to introduce me as the new Customer Service Excellence Champion (I know, the job title didn't exactly roll off the tongue!). Like everyone else there that day, it was the first I'd heard of my new role, and while I shrunk under the glare of the crowd, he explained to everyone how I would be working with each department, under the remit 'to create moments of delight'.

I became Iain's protégé from that moment, and it is no exaggeration to say that it did change my life. I was, by then, 17-years old, still doing my A-Levels, working 50-hours a week at Sandy Balls: but earning a fortune in cash and commercial knowhow. They threatened to kick me out of sixth-form because my attendance was so poor. However, my grades were still OK, and, as a cross-department customer service consultant, my real-world business education was far beyond anything a classroom could deliver. My average working day saw me working alongside the restaurant managers, the leisure centre, in the pub, entertainment services, events teams, guest services, a shop, and the sales and marketing departments. I knew I had landed on my feet because I was earning while learning, but at that age, I don't think you fully understand how valuable that sort of experience can be.

Despite my part-time, drowsy-eyed attendance, my college grades were good enough to land me a place at Bournemouth University doing a Business Management degree, and Iain was happy for me to combine study with work. The first day on campus arrived, and I pitched the same splitting of my time and resources proposal to the teaching staff. They stared at me silently, looked at one another curiously and, without a single word passing between them, delivered their unified decision. In short, they weren't too impressed with the idea, suggesting I hadn't understood the depth or nature of the course, and it quickly became apparent negotiation wasn't an option. It turns out that a full-time university degree means what it says on the form.

My one-day residence at Bournemouth University taught me a valuable lesson. Status quo stifles opportunity, and the traditional school, to sixth-form, to university roadmap, is not the only way to success. I have since learned that the 'you have to go to university' mantra preached to all promising students is a noisy lie that encourages brilliance to keep its head below the opportunity parapet for years longer than necessary. I am not saying don't go – simply suggesting young people should ask themselves why – or what is their bigger picture. Like the marketing stereotype (or dying breed) I want to challenge in this book, students need to look at the broader picture and see that the majority's path only leads to being average. That is not a slur on anyone; it is a simple fact: the majority 'by definition' is also the average.

Discovering sales

I don't think Iain was at all surprised to see me back in his office that day, and he quickly agreed to put me through an Open University degree instead. The new arrangement meant increasing my work/ study hours to 90-per-week, but it was entirely on my terms because I had chosen to do it and was entirely in line with the direction I wanted to go.

As tends to happen when you are busy, time went quickly, and the day soon arrived when Iain called me into his office and asked me what I wanted to do. I was now nineteen, had completed my degree, and I guess he thought I needed to specialise and hone my skills rather than continue spreading myself throughout the business. I chose marketing and took a role as a junior copywriter, writing emails and leaflet content, organising flyer drops, updating the brochure, photocopying and general admin. One day a call came through saying the sales department was short and needed an extra body to voice phones. I was the obvious choice because I had a broad knowledge of the business and had worked in and around the sales team. I would also have done anything to escape another day of leaflet collating at that point.

The role I was standing in for meant answering phone enquiries or taking bookings for holidays. It turned out they were simply looking for someone to help manage the number of calls and ensure customers were not kept waiting at busy times of the day (an initiative I had suggested during my Customer Service Excellence Champion days). But it quickly became apparent that no one had ever considered the possibility of turning enquiries into sales or upselling sales to premium bookings. And here is the interesting thing, looking back on it now with my ex-salesperson's eyes, no one told me that selling was part of the role. I am proud that I never felt the need to knock on Iain's door and tell him what I was doing, but my sales figures soon won the manager's and eventually his attention.

We live in a competitive world, and I have since learned that you need to shout about yourself to stand out from the crowd occasionally, but I also know that nothing speaks louder than doing a great job and showing you have genuine value to offer. Noise does get people's attention in the short term, but smart leaders recognise talent.

You don't necessarily need to shout about it; that is a lesson worth remembering. If you are reading this book as a marketer, I would urge you to be innovative, be creative and break the mould – take chances and show the people you work for that proper marketing does more than ticking boxes. And if you are reading this book as a salesperson, board member or owner of a business – please don't let talent and innovation die or go somewhere – go and find out what your marketing people are capable of achieving.

Within a few months, I became the assistant sales manager, despite being half the age of almost every other team member, and when the manager left, I took over the department. There were twelve people in the sales team by that time, ranging from school-leavers to mums working part-time, and we were breaking sales records month after month. Sales became my passion and managing that diverse group of individuals was highly educational. It gave me a fantastic insight into people, their motivations, priorities, and propensity to absorb and develop new skills. I also learned a lot about myself over that period.

Moving-on

Remember the moving-on arrow in the Marketer's Hierarchy of Needs model? My situation was not exactly the same as that because Iain recognised my potential perhaps more than I did. But I had certainly reached a ceiling in that business and one where I could not move any further forward. It was not that the board were stopping me from advancing – there simply was nowhere to go.

I was a go-getter; my mind was always on, thinking of new things to try and looking for opportunities to sell more holidays and activities to more people. Every day I would knock on Iain's door with a suggestion or an idea to shake up or challenge the team. I don't know how he took the constant interruptions, but eventually, even I got tired of my enthusiasm. As the daily knocks became weekly ones and my passion dissolved into working hard, paying the bills and relaxing at home ready for the next day, something snapped. And on one of my, by then infrequent visits to Iain's office, he said to me, "Rich, you've gone all pipe and slippers". I was twenty-one years old.

That day I went home, told my then fiancé I was moving to London and started searching and applying for sales jobs before even arriving at work with my resignation letter the following morning. She was not impressed and made it quite clear that living in the big city, away from all she had ever known in the safe, samey, certainty of the New Forest, was not part of her life plan. I am only mildly embarrassed to admit that our decision to ditch future wedding plans over an ambitious career move was an easy one. There was never any regret on my part, and although more romantically-minded readers may think it was a heartless act, the same logic would suggest it saved prolonging a more painful separation. The board at Sandy Balls were far more understanding and supportive, and they agreed I could work an open-ended notice until I found the right role. (I'm not sure my fiancé would have agreed to such terms.) Iain gave me one last piece of solid advice: don't accept the first job offered. I was so eager to get out of there, I completely ignored him and moved into London to start a new life one week after that initial offer arrived.

So here is the thing that surprised me the most. Having already had several experiences of arriving in a new environment, thinking I would have to learn from those who were already doing the role yet quickly finding myself leading the pack, the same thing happened again. I don't say this to brag or make out that I instinctively know it all, but to reinforce my earlier point. The majority are, by default, average. And if you, in whatever role you find yourself today, do have even an inkling that you can do better, I want to encourage you to put yourself out there and be the best. Go and stand out by showing average what outstanding looks like.

Soon after joining that long-established, respected, large, and to be perfectly frank, second-rate publishing company, I realised my mistake. I have no doubt they must have done something right at some point in their history. But they had become so inflexible and unwilling to listen to the market, their customers, or a host of good people who wanted to change the business model from the inside; it was clear there was little hope. The nine months I spent there were some of the most painful and infuriating of my life, and I have never felt so ineffective due to ignorance and stupidity of decisions from outside of my direct control. I will not go into the details or even name the company (you are welcome to try and guess), but I will tell you how my relationship with that organisation ended. After announcing I was going to leave (and I may have let it slip that I had an offer), I was locked in a room – quite literally – while someone rapidly drew up a contract and insisted I could not leave until I had signed to say I would not join Raconteur. I knew they couldn't keep me in that room, but the door genuinely was locked, and Arsenal was on TV that night, so eventually, I signed their pointless piece of paper 'M. Mouse' and moved on.

And as I left their premises for the last time, smiling at the fact no one had even bothered to decipher my squiggle, I thought to myself, "do you want sauce with that?"

CHAPTER 6

Inside the
salesperson's psyche.

Do you remember, in chapter three, I promised you a full apology for being a salesperson? Well, this chapter is that apology, although at no point will I actually say the word 'sorry'. Why? Because I am from a sales background and I do believe I am always right – it is part of my nature and what makes me good at my job. My apology will arrive in the form of an insight into how a salesperson's mind and motivation work and what makes them the brash, insensitive, impatient, overconfident and occasionally downright rude individuals they tend to be. And why should you care about understanding salespeople better? Because sales mean income, income (should) generate profit, and profit fuels business growth, pays everyone's wages, and (as my good friend Philipus always reminds me) keeps us all in a job. Yes, I know that is a narrow salesperson's view; everyone else plays their role too, and the sales team alone does not make a business tick, but they do provide the lifeblood that keeps every company alive – revenue.

As a salesperson who now runs a marketing agency, my experience tells me as loud as any message I have learned in my career that sales and marketing working in perfect harmony guarantees increased revenue. And I also know that revenue will increase even more dramatically if marketing's voice is allowed to influence (or even dictate) sales and board-level strategy. Most salespeople would laugh at me for that statement, but I vehemently believe it.

Why? Because it is true.

We will come to the second of those ideal scenarios later in the book, but we cannot address that until we have fixed the first – the ever-widening divide. The bottom line is that marketers will never claim the place where we can be most effective while feeling sorry for ourselves, bowing to the status quo or begrudging our big bully of a cousin. That is why this chapter is about understanding who salespeople really are and opening the door to help them help you, themselves and the bigger picture.

I know I started the last paragraph stating my credentials as a salesperson, and ended this one claiming a place in marketing. That is because sales is in my blood and part of my nature, but marketing has captured my heart and fundamentally changed my core beliefs.

Setting your sights on sales

Salespeople are pretty single-minded in their thinking about work. They have one primary objective, and that is to close as many deals as possible. They only care about the detail if it closes more deals; statistics and tech stacks will only matter if they help close deals. They will only be nice to customer services, marketing, HR, accounts or any other department if doing so will push more deals over the line. Trying to change that basic, carnal mentality is like asking a lion to go vegetarian; time to start moving backwards; or an Arsenal fan to support Spurs. I would add the caveat here that this description only refers to the best salespeople; mediocre ones lack the rabid hunger that drives them to achieve the purpose of being a salesperson – more sales. It is critical to understand this foundation principle because it frames every decision, action, interaction and willingness to stop and listen in a salesperson's day.

A successful salesperson's life consists of high risk, high reward, fast decisions and quick wins. They would score a three or, at best, a four on the perfectionist's scale and live by the unshakeable belief that 'good enough is good enough' (which it always is, if you really think about the words). Salespeople are rarely well educated – you will notice how sales only ever forms part of other business degrees and doesn't have one entirely of its own. (Based on a two-minute Google search at the time of writing – but it seems they bring out new-fangled degrees every five minutes, so that may change.) Salespeople dream about closing sales, worry about unclosed deals in the evenings or at weekends, get suspicious and defensive if competitors come up in conversation and hate the very concept of rejection (even though they face it every day). Is it any wonder that salespeople are often on edge, distracted or deliver an irritated snap when you ask them (what they consider to be) an irrelevant question in a moment when you think they are simply taking in the view outside the window?

To put it another way, if I were to create a Salesperson's Hierarchy of Needs, it would not be a pyramid at all – it would be a continual circle with the words risk (in red) and reward (in green), repeating all around its circumference. Ninety-five per cent of a salesperson's life is not glamour, praise and bonuses as you might suppose. It is stress and hard work. Their confidence is just the armour they wear; their arrogance is primarily circumstantial; and their reluctance to slow down, listen to or learn from others (particularly the marketing department) results from fearing for their next sale, target or job. Salespeople are survivors, fighters and self-obsessed lone-riders. They often see their peers as competition as much as they do the actual competition, and if there is a shortcut that will save them time, even if it comes with fifty-fifty odds of blowing up in their face, they are likely to take it in a heartbeat. Such is the enhanced self-confidence of a high-achieving salesperson; they would always see fifty-fifty odds as eighty-twenty in their favour anyway.

Let me give you a few more generalisations of the psyche and modus operandi of the people strutting around your sales department before I explain how these insights can help heal the rift.

Salespeople rarely embrace technology unless it can be proven to save them time, close more deals, or make their lives easier. And, of course, even then, only under the proviso that someone else sets the tech up for them and can explain how to use it in plain English in under three minutes. If they have a system that works; a pen and notepad, their over-crowded email inbox or an Excel spreadsheet for the more modern, they will resist the need for change. I know salespeople who still use Rolodex card files despite their company spending tens of thousands developing a bespoke CRM system to manage their pipeline.

Scott Allen, Global Marketing Strategy Director for Microsoft, says, *"During our marketing transformation project within Microsoft, we started taking our salespeople on a story: how we used to do marketing, where one touchpoint equated to one lead and represented a victory for marketing if the sale came through. We then describe how we use technology to capture customer signals and activities to gain intelligent insights so we can serve up Highly Engaged Accounts."* He explains, *"We now go to the salespeople with greater insight, making us more relevant to them, and they are responding positively by identifying marketings influential role on the sale."*

My point is that you won't attract a salesperson's attention because you know what is good for them any more than you will persuade a teenager that going to bed early instead of staying up playing computer games is good for them. You have to sell them the story. If you want to show salespeople marketing is more than just events, give-aways and goodies, you must prove to them that insights, analytics and understanding the touchpoints through smart digital marketing and technology works. You don't need to be afraid of their reaction if you are confident that you can help them do their job. You just need to understand their motivations.

Despite the go-go-go persona I have just described, the best salespeople are actually quite good at managing and compartmentalising their time. They have to be because there are so many different elements demanding their time in their high-pressure existence: cold-calling, listening, pitching, chasing, closing, listening, spinning, smiling, responding, outreach, listening, explaining, presenting, and repeating. And the only thing common to every single one of these activities is the salesperson's least popular word – No! I mentioned it earlier, but it is a fact that no other profession is so full of the one thing the professional doing that job hates most of all. In this case, it is rejection. It is a wonder that these people even come into work or muster the energy and fortitude to wander around the office like they own the place while looking down their noses at lesser employees whose roles they have no interest in trying to understand.

Listen, my desire in writing this chapter is not to make you feel sorry for salespeople. (In fact, it might have had the opposite effect and confirmed what you already believed.) And I doubt I have achieved much sympathy anyway; perhaps that is what you would expect from a salesperson spouting self-indulgent, stereotypical exaggerations for comedic effect or to win your approval. What I really want to do is paint a picture of someone who is the polar opposite, in most respects, to the people who work in marketing departments (or any other department for that matter). And that brings me to one last point to consider when digging beneath the surface of the salesperson's psyche. They know that HR, finance, procurement, logistics, administration and marketing do not like them very much, which only adds to the pressure they feel to perform.

Spinning the sales team

One of the salesperson's favourite techniques is SPIN selling. It is simple, seamless, and, once perfected, will uncover potential opportunities like nothing else I know. If you haven't read the best selling book by Nick Rackham, it goes something like this:

SITUATION. This is where you set the scene, discuss the current situation and draw out a comprehensive picture of where the prospect is with their current arrangement, product or service.

PROBLEM. Next, you create a 'what if?' moment by suggesting a potential but likely and realistic problem for the prospect to consider. It could be a hole you have spotted in the current situation, or you might even conjure up some hypothetical issues that could occur in the future. And remember, two or three problems are better than one.

IMPLICATION. This is the most influential stage of the SPIN framework, where you amplify the potential problems you've highlighted. You do this by switching attention to the aftermath and consequences of the problem and the implications caused to the current situation, the business and most importantly, the individual you are selling to.

NEED. If you have successfully negotiated S, P and I in the sales model, you will have created a need in the heart and mind of your prospect. All the salesperson needs to do now is explain how their solution will stop the situation from ever becoming a problem in the first place. You have uncovered a need your prospect didn't know they had, and you have sold them the solution.

If you are unfamiliar with SPIN selling, you will either be thinking how clever or sneaky it is or maybe that the two-hundred and twelve words I used to describe a method it takes years to perfect sounds easy. I promise you it is none of those things. It is simply a process to describe the art of understanding another person's needs (including potential unspoken or unidentified weaknesses, flaws and gaps in their knowledge or ability) and helping them find a solution. It is not sneaky or dishonest because the need is always real; it is just that the prospect needs help to recognise its existence. SPIN selling is about asking questions, listening to answers, empathising with emotions, and acknowledging that people do not know what you know. And it is a powerful tool for changing minds, opening the door for relationships to begin and finding solutions for the situations people often don't realise they need help to solve.

Let me recap my position here and my reason for writing this book. I am a salesperson with a successful sales career who has found himself running a marketing agency – and loving every minute. When

I was in an active sales role, I would say unkind, disrespectful and unwarranted things about marketing people both behind closed doors and boldly in any open room. I could blame youthful exuberance, any of the factors detailed in this chapter so far, or simple ignorance, but it won't change the fact that I was an idiot – I was wrong. My experience working with marketers over the last few years and in my current role has led to understanding this was not only wrong, but it was also naive, and it has highlighted for me both the problem and the solution. Sales departments unequivocally need the help of marketing departments; more to the point, the entire business function needs marketing's skills, insight and wisdom, but they don't recognise that they do.

And the only people who can open their eyes to the bottom line, the bigger picture, are marketing people. It is up to marketing to put themselves in a place where they can make a difference because no one else has a strong enough motivation to change the status quo. Everyone else is doing OK and getting the respect and recognition they deserve – marketing is facing cutbacks, assimilation or annihilation.

Marketing to the sales team

As I implied earlier, it takes years to perfect SPIN selling and having a salesperson's personality helps too, so I am not suggesting marketing starts schmoozing. But marketing people do have all the tools, skills and temperament needed to change the landscape and reverse the gap between the two critical sales functions that create profitable revenue for a business. They just need to add a little spin to how they market the idea.

I have described how I see the situation and whether you agree with me entirely or not, you have read this far, so I must have touched a nerve. The problem is that salespeople do not care about marketing's predicament or recognise that it affects them in the long run. They think, as I did, that marketing moves too slow, gets caught up in details, generates pages of boring collateral no one will read, cares more about the aesthetics than the needs the customers want them to address, and doesn't live in the real world. They also think the leads marketing passes across are unqualified, irrelevant or just plain weak. And therein lies the main problem I want to highlight as we close this chapter. The one place where sales and marketing will always come together and brush against the other's side, regardless of how operationally distant they become, is the handover of leads. In most cases, that is the weakest link in the revenue generation chain where all the angst, mistrust and opinions begin.

So let's spin the lead argument on its head. First, stop thinking of them as leads. If you ask a salesperson what a good lead looks like, they will say, "give me someone I can sell to". They mean, give me someone who is open to a conversation about the products and services I have to sell, or in salesperson's language: someone with a need. This simple understanding is *so* potent because you can bypass the situation and problem and imply a solution (satisfy the need) by reframing the question.

Picture the scene. A marketer asks a salesperson who they would like to have a conversation with and what that conversation might sound like. The salesperson gives them an answer, and the marketer (taking notes) says, "So, if I could find ten people like that over the next two or three months, would that be a good result for you?" I know that sounds unrealistic and perhaps oversimplistic, but can you see how something like that would start to change the dynamic and the relationship between these two partners in creating revenue? It would certainly hold more weight and generate a stronger understanding than delivering data that sales won't read, collateral they think is unusable and leads they don't rate.

I have laid out the situation and highlighted a crucial issue that needs to be addressed to help heal the sales and marketing divide. We also looked briefly at how marketing might imply and present the need or solution. I want to stress again that this is not a book about sales versus marketing, but before moving toward the real value I have for you, we need to explore the communication gap a little more and teach marketing to at least meet sales halfway.

CHAPTER 7

Be more purple.

You will be familiar with personality profiling models, such as the DISC or Myers Briggs systems. Which of us hasn't scanned the multiple-choice looking for answers that make us seem less like a psychopath or tried second-guessing what the person over the desk is looking for in an interview? Cynicism aside, the science is quite compelling, and I challenge you to look through the various descriptions and not see friends, family, colleagues (and, of course, your own best attributes) staring back. I say 'best' attributes because no one likes having their faults highlighted, do they? If you are unfamiliar with the science, here is a summary:

A hundred years of research, most notably that of William Moulton Marston in the early 1900s, have concluded four primary personality types: red, yellow, green, and blue. History tells us this principle has existed in other formats long before that, going back to the Greeks, the Aztecs and other major civilisations. The latest science says that 80% of us are a mixture of two colours (a predominant and a secondary), 15% invite a third shade onto their personality palate, and 5% display an entirely singular hue in their approach to life. Each profile has distinct attributes, affecting their strengths, weaknesses, emotions, motivations and communication style. And you'll not be surprised to learn that most salespeople have strong tendencies towards red behaviour.

Red characteristics. These people like to dominate any room. They are direct, decisive, usually in a hurry and don't need anyone else's permission to make decisions. In fact, they will resist being told how to do anything because they already know best. Other personality types view them as egotistical or arrogant and avoid getting into a discussion or argument because they know they won't win. Red people are risk-takers, embrace change and enjoy a challenge – especially if there is a reward at the end.

Yellow characteristics. These are the bouncy people in your life. They give you the benefit of the doubt, are always optimistic, talk too much and show emotion at the drop of a hat. As team players, yellow people will encourage others, try and make you laugh and always be the first to present a creative idea or solution. Non-yellow people often see them as fluffy and shallow, poor listeners and easily offended. Yellow people love praise and thrive in a happy environment where everyone gets on and is supportive.

Green characteristics. These are the seen-not-heard types. They are steady, friendly, proud perfectionists and totally dependable – almost to a fault. Rules and compliance underpin everything they do, and they are empathetic, patient listeners. Other people might see them as weak, sensitive and too restricted by their resistance to change or new ideas. Green people love long term security, taking life at a slow and predictable pace and seeing a project through from start to finish with no loose ends.

Blue characteristics. These are the conscientious analysts. They read statistics and data like other people read sentences and are obsessively systematic about their work. Facts are the most critical feature of any discussion for a blue. Opinions about those facts or how they might make people feel have little consequence to the conclusions they draw. People without blue in their profile tend to view them as narrow-minded, inflexible and too bound by the rules. Blue people tend to be very serious and lack a sense of humour, although, in reality, they simply have a different idea of what is funny.

Of course, these are generalisms, and I do not want to go too deep into the science of personality profiling, as I am certainly no expert in the field. But I do see that the different types exist, and it only takes a little knowledge of the principles involved to recognise the main traits and gently pigeonhole everyone you know.

In his delightfully titled book, 'Surrounded by Idiots', Swedish behavioural expert Thomas Erikson applies the science of personality profiling to communication and examines how these types converse with and tolerate (or not) each other. It is a fascinating study, and one of the main points I drew from it was accepting that everyone is different. It is not a yellow person's fault they always try to be upbeat; a blue person cannot help boring others with data; you cannot blame a green person for not commenting when they have nothing to add; and if a red person talks to you like you are an idiot, it is just the way they are. You can disagree all you like and accuse red people of being rude, blue obsessive, green dull, and yellow just annoying, but it won't do any good. The gene pool and life circumstances, nature and nurture, have made us all what we are, and there is little anyone can do about changing something as deep-rooted as personality.

It takes effort, empathy and a willingness to understand for relationships to improve and trust to grow. But knowledge is power, and we can adapt our own behaviours – if we want to. I first learned these rules as a salesperson, but now as a business leader, I default to personality profiling every time I walk into a room. It just works: and I have found the more I understand the nature of the individuals I am talking to, the more effective and persuasive I can be in my communication with them.

Ironically, salespeople, who as 'reds' are typically the most aggressively stereotyped of all the profiles, are excellent communicators and adaptors when they are selling. If they are building rapport, executing a spin or being interested in what their prospective customer did over the weekend to help close a deal, they will pull an Oscar-winning performance out of the bag. It is only back in the office and among people who are less valuable than customers that the redness returns. Perhaps I am a little harsh to salespeople there, but remember my observation in the last chapter about salespeople being singular in their approach to work? Their primary objective is to close more deals, and they are under immense pressure to hit targets and keep their jobs, so they will always prioritise and adapt to those circumstances. It is not their fault.

As we discussed before, salespeople are often blind to the fact that marketing people are, in fact, the best friends they have in the entire organisation. A good marketer has access to more business intelligence, market trends, buying patterns and customer painpoints than anyone else. The problem is that they present it to salespeople in the form of data and analysis. Salespeople are blind to that form of communication – they simply do not care. When presenting tech stacks and pages of detail, marketing departments are driving the wedge between them and sales even deeper instead of drawing these powerful allies towards each other.

Yes, salespeople can often display what might come across as bullying behaviours or a superiority complex that can undermine marketers, and I am not justifying this on any level. But this is a psychological barrier that marketing people have to overcome. And, although the one place where marketers can feel totally dominant and superior to sales is technology, data and digital everything, my strong advice to marketers is to resist the urge to beat sales at their own misguided game and try to make them feel inferior. You may win that battle, but you will not be doing any favours to the peace that will bring about prosperity for all.

Nurturing the blind

Let me share with you one of my most significant eye-opening moments of the last few years. It was 2017, and many memorable things happened: Trump took office in the USA, Theresa May signed Article 50, committing the UK to Brexit; Arsenal won the FA Cup for the thirteenth time, and I finally realised why salespeople need to understand the marketing nurturing process.

It was February, and I was in a barren sales period for one of the first times in my career. It was an uncomfortable feeling. The competition was more demanding than ever, disruptive trends such as personalisation were on the rise, and GDPR put the whole sales and marketing funnel under immense pressure. It seemed that restrictions were all designed to make selling more complicated and more of a slog. Looking back now, I think I went into 'looking for someone to blame' mode and ended up at the marketing department's door. We had numerous conversations, with me pushing for a campaign that worked instantly and generated quick-win leads to go and talk to, while they countered that an approach like that would kill the pipeline for six months down the track. Fortunately for me, my marketing department was being more purple on that occasion, and instead of giving in to my demands for a quick result, I agreed to let them explain the bigger picture. After all, for once, I had time on my hands with nothing to follow up or chase. Through gritted teeth and still carrying a degree of cynicism, I set about understanding how the marketing team were attracting and nurturing prospects towards the lip of the sales funnel.

Suddenly, it was like someone handed me a pair of colourblindness correction glasses. (Please stop reading for a moment and search 'kids given glasses' on YouTube.) My eyes were open, and I started to see the intricacies of how marketing works. The method, the depth of thought and design, the long-term strategy, the focus on understanding the market first, careful attention to research, response and trends, and, most importantly, the nurturing process: lead grading, lead scoring, and personalisation. I remember thinking how, if I'd known this earlier, I wouldn't have been so generic in my own outreach, and I could have saved myself time scampering around, searching for relevant pieces of collateral and wasting so many opportunities on futile conversations and tasks. I was both embarrassed at my tunnel vision and a little bit annoyed with the marketing department for not showing their purple side more often – I am red after all, and it is hard to change your nature. This book was born from that experience in many ways because it launched a more hand-in-hand, equal status and full-respect approach to selling within our business.

At a subsequent B2B marketing round table meeting, our marketing operations manager reported a dramatically improved rate for closing deals by making lead scoring much simpler and showing the sales team exactly what actions a prospect had taken. They had not changed a single thing about how they did the work, just how they communicated the results to the sales team. She said, "We made the whole process more transparent and engaging, and the sales team have flown". What struck me was the pride and almost red-level sense of achievement at proving their contribution emanating from her smile and voice.

As a salesperson, it is so clear now that a deep understanding of the lead nurture process will help close more deals. Clarity over the route a prospect has sailed before entering the sales pipeline means you can tailor your approach to the opening conversation, access the customer's previous interactions, create a personalised approach and start the conversation with a winning hand. And instead of risking confused messages and crossed wires about the solution on offer, the tone of the sales discussion will remain consistent and on track. Since then, we have proactively increased open communication and consolidated goals and targets between marketing and sales in our business. Measuring the results and data shows that successful sales are three times more likely before the salesperson has even met the prospect – a powerful statement for the marketing department. We can see how there has been a dialogue with our brand at multiple points before they have spoken to a real person; the tone and message of that dialogue are now perfectly in tune with the salesperson's approach to the conversation when they take over the baton. So, the first contact with a salesperson should feel like a continuation of the original dialogue, not a cold call.

The more we saw this approach making a difference, the more we realised the need to formalise and structure the process. So we now run clearly defined service level agreements (SLAs) to measure and monitor the inputs and expectations of the two sides of the nurture to pipeline equation. The SLA specifies both strategy and tactics for marketing and the sales activities that will convert leads into sales. And it also clarifies points of contact and actions if the plan starts veering off track.

The internal conversation between marketing and sales is now open, honest and equally two-way. So we can continually fine-tune the process and make intelligent decisions on every lead that enters the funnel: should it be discarded, or does it need a little more nurturing? This one simple change in approach has changed the entire dynamic of marketing and sales in our business and helped us identify other abrasive areas, miscommunications and bottlenecks in the process. The confirmation bias now dictates that sales and marketing are partners, equals, and part of the organisation's same progressive, revenue-generating function.

If you look back at the story, you would be perfectly correct to accuse sales of being the problem, and that may well be true. But in most organisations, sales is not the department under threat of extinction-level change. And we have already established that sales (due to nature and self-survival instinct) are unlikely to change. So the onus lies on marketing to change (to wake up and fulfil their self-survival instinct). In my experience, marketers tend to be mostly green personality types, perhaps with a splash of blue or yellow. And while a good characteristic of green people is their consistency, dependability and thoroughness, those tendencies can also manifest as stubbornness. If you are a professional marketer reading this book now, I urge you not to be stubborn or proud about this issue. Yes, it may well be salespeople's delusions of self-importance that caused the problem, but only your willingness and ability to understand the situation and communicate a solution can turn it around. Do what you are good at! Present a marketing solution and be more purple.

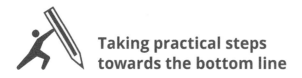

Taking practical steps towards the bottom line

Once you have considered the individual personality traits - you also need to remember how Sales and Marketing generally see the world. On the right is a good representation originally produced by global research firm B2B International.

SALES	SUBJECT	MARKETING
I have a product which I need to move. My aim is to persuade someone to buy it.	**PRODUCT**	I have a range of products and my aim is to ensure it meets customer's needs.
Price can often be my biggest stumbling block. Wherever I go, buyers tell me that our prices are higher than our competitors.	**PRICE**	My aim is to capture value, to understand what people want and what they will pay for. I want to ensure we don't leave money on the table.
Promotions that focus on the product and promise a discount are, in my opinion, the most effective.	**PROMOTION**	Promotions should resonate with the target audience, which includes anyone who has an influence on the buying decision.
Most of the time I like to speak to the buyer – the person who places the order. I am normally dealing one-to-one.	**AUDIENCE**	My audience can be broad, including specifiers, buyers, influencers and ranging from the user on the shop floor through to the people in the C-suite.
I'm judged on weekly and monthly sales. I have to get the product out of the door quickly.	**TIME HORIZON**	I take a long-term view and am always thinking of where the business will be in a year or two.
I am the face of the company. When people think of the company they think of me. I am the brand.	**BRAND REPUTATION**	I see the brand as a unique position for our company. If we can build such a position, it will be hard for competitors to take it away from us.
My strategy is to push product out of the door. After all, that is my job; I am a sales person.	**STRATEGY**	My strategy is to pull customers towards a company. I want to draw them in so they are highly interested in us as a company and the products we supply.

CHAPTER 8

Knowing the customer behind the data.

People have debated the sales and marketing divide to death over the years, and I am well aware my thoughts on the matter over the last few chapters depend on bravery, stepping outside comfort zones and willingness from both sides to engage. That is easier said than done, but nothing worth fighting for is a quick fix or without its challenges. And this is a cause that we must win. I also know from my own experiences that collaboration is only possible through open communication, understanding your partner's position, and agreeing on a common goal that is the best outcome for everyone. And, while it was critical to highlight the relationship between sales and marketing and suggest a solution, I want to stress again that this book is not about that fight. It is about putting marketing in a position where it can recognise its own value and then promote that commercial worth to the decision-makers who are missing out on its potential. Ultimately, this is a win-win-win pitch for sales, marketing and the business in its entirety.

Getting sales onside is only part of the equation. I would refer you back to the 'move on' arrow in the Marketer's Hierarchy of Needs model at this point because I truly believe that getting stuck on the 'security' level is sentencing yourself to a slow demise. If you want to shine and no one is listening, please consider moving to an organisation that will listen. With that in mind, in this chapter, we will drill deeper into the opportunities at a marketing department's fingertips (as they get closer to sales and the rest of the business) and identify some practical ways to increase and utilise that capability.

I have mentioned how marketing departments are well-equipped to drive strategy because of their unrivalled access and ability to interrogate data. The problem with this data, however, is that it is just that – data. I think it was Dwight Eisenhower who famously said, *"No plan survives first contact with the enemy"*. Meaning that all the analysis, data, past performance and future predictions were critical to reaching the battle line, but the real fight only begins when the first shot rings out. Then, it is all about the frontline activity, clear communication lines to and from the command centre and getting the right supplies and support into the field as quickly as possible.

Likewise, customer research and market trends are vitally important to creating a campaign and building a nurturing process, but conversations with customers are where the real action happens. While SLAs between sales and marketing departments must include feedback from pitches, cold calls, outreach and onboarding conversations, nothing is more valuable than a marketing person in the room when sales conversations happen. I am not suggesting marketing people become salespeople here – let's not get ahead of ourselves. But I firmly believe that a marketer who spends more time in and around their sales team, talking to them, learning from them, experiencing what they do in their world, and meeting your (collective) prospects and customers face-to-face is walking in gold dust. When I talk to marketers about this idea, nine out of ten tell me they would like to make that move, but, to be honest, few of them ever do. I urge you to stop talking about it and be more purple.

Yes, the reverse is also true. A salesperson who spends time understanding the nurturing process, appreciating the patience required to see a campaign through, and learning the value in the data will be equally better off for the experience. But remember, sales do not need to change – they are still closing deals, earning bonuses and claiming respect. I have probably laboured this point so far, but I simply cannot stress it strongly enough. If marketing makes the first move and proves that they can help close deals (as our marketing team did at Raconteur), the sales department will notice. And in return, they will become more open to deeper collaborations, other joined-up working initiatives and invites to spend time in each other's worlds. You will be amazed how quickly single-minded people respond to the one thing that matters to them most when you SPIN them a compelling, evidence-based story.

Rational decisions based on emotional understanding

Let's dig a little deeper into the value of getting in front of customers, putting faces to the numbers and emotion to the raw data. The mantra 'people buy people' has been handed down through generations because it is true. But it is not just true in the domain of sales; it applies to every aspect of life and relationship building: from getting on with your boss to finding your soulmate or who you choose to cut your hair. The adverts that live longest in our minds are personal, filled with people like us, and designed to touch emotions. TV channels and video sharing platforms bombard us with people stories, life journeys and every type of reality show they have yet to imagine. And among all of this people-flavoured emotional engagement, the marketing companies collect data, analyse tastes, track spending and identify trends. But that is the point where the big mistake often happens. The analysts forget the data they are reading is all about emotional people who respond best to other emotional people. The only way to truly understand your customers is to get in front of them and talk to them: to understand their pain points and challenges. You can gauge a massive amount from the data, but ultimately people will always buy people. So far in this book, I have spoken to you as an ex-salesperson who runs a marketing agency – let me speak to you as a buyer who influences significant buying decisions for his company. I almost always choose products and solutions because of the people I speak with, over and above the product's reputation, the service's track record or the advert I saw on social media.

"I think we can sometimes approach B2B marketing as a corporate, talking to a corporate, and in reality, certainly in professional services, we are humans talking to humans," says Annabel Rake, CMO at Deloitte UK and South and North Europe. *"And I think we sometimes use corporate-speak (words you wouldn't necessarily use in everyday language) in our marketing, to put forward our communications in a rational, data-based way. That can work to a point, as there are certainly people who benefit from and engage with data. But I think we forget we are talking to people and people engage in emotional ways."*

A report by Peter Field and Les Binet, authors of the book, The Long and Short of It: Balancing Short and Long-Term Marketing Strategies, compared emotional marketing campaigns against those built around rational data. They found that rational campaigns were effective in short-term transactional situations, while emotional campaigns were seven times more powerful in generating long-term impact for businesses. This probably won't come as much of a surprise to most readers, but the conclusion is massively important. How can you engage on an emotional, personal, human level if all you do is interrogate the data and never talk to the people? And the problem is that most marketing people do not get to talk to customers and prospects directly, so all the critical emotional evaluations get smothered out by the spreadsheet or tech stack.

Annabel Rake went on to say, *"We ask clients at the end of a bid process, successful or unsuccessful, what won us or lost us the work or enabled a competitor to win? They usually tell us they are selecting on rational points, such as services, cost or value. But when we dig deeper beneath the data, it shows that it is actually things like a client team coming across as dynamic, hungry and passionate for the work and building rapport with the client. We win more often when those human emotional attributes are displayed. When you first see the data, you look at the rational stuff, and you naturally think it is about the service and the cost we're putting forward. Of course, there are elements of that in any bid. But I think when you dig deeper below the surface, you see that there's a bit more to it than that".*

In the second half of this book, we will look at revolutionising marketing's approach to budgets, campaigns and measuring the effectiveness of its bottom-line contribution to the business. I have used the word 'revolutionise', but in many ways, I am pointing at a return to the original definition, purpose, and operational strategies marketing employed decades ago. I believe the future of marketing can be exciting and business-shaping. Marketers can become the superstars in their organisations (like they were in the glory days of marketing when its creative campaigns really did change the world) and dictate their own terms.

I am pushing for a paradigm shift, and that means uncomfortable change is necessary. And if marketing departments are not prepared to take the first step and become more engaged with frontline customer engagement, there is little hope for what needs to happen beyond that.

Revenue is the best read headline in the business

Here is an uncomfortable truth that may be difficult for marketers to hear. Salespeople regularly (and secretly) create their own marketing collateral because they believe the brochures, adverts, webinars and blogs their marketing departments give them are not relevant to their prospects. I don't want to get into the rights and wrongs of this practice because I have been guilty of doing the same and would defend it in some cases. But I know one thing for sure: even if the sales version has a more relevant message, it will always be of poorer quality, probably off-brand and certainly out of sync with other activities marketing is trying to push. Salespeople will often contradict the contents of their own company's collateral. They will look surprised at seeing marketing material for the first time on a customer's desk or disguise a shake of the head as they bluff past a detail that is irrelevant (in their opinion) to the prospect in front of them.

Once again, the problem highlighted here is two-sided, and you could easily argue that sales are in the wrong. But opening the door of internal communication, understanding the common objectives and customer requirements, and agreeing on a joined-up approach would solve the issue. Marketing must start engaging with the frontline sales process for this to happen. They can then create quality collateral that is relevant and effective for sales to close more deals. When this happens, everyone wins, more doors open internally and externally, and marketing will start to grab headlines in the corridors of sales self-talk. To push in the same direction, allies need to agree on what direction they want to face.

For marketing to take its rightful place as a strategic lead in today's organisations, it needs to grab the headlines. That means demonstrating how it directly influences the revenue that a company generates. Typically, their focus moves from building the brand to accumulating views to generating leads and then feeding the pipeline – and that is where the story ends. So, the existing process in most organisations cannot prove the value of marketing's efforts because the revenue only appears after sales have closed the deal. It is like the speedy, silky skills of a talented midfielder ghosting past three defenders and placing an inch-perfect cross for the waiting goal-hungry striker to tap it in the goal. We've all seen such scenarios played out hundreds of times on football fields all over the world. Who does the rest of the team congratulate first? Who do the fans adore? But when the cross is too long or too short, the commentators defend the star striker, observing how they are left feeding on scraps today.

Life is unfair sometimes, but good managers know their team and recognise their strengths. Likewise, a true team with honest, hard-working team players, who have an equal desire to win, appreciate the internal efforts of every team player, the coaching staff and the medical team. But the key to building a successful team always begins with identifying the end goal first and then recognising contributions.

In sport, lifting trophies is the end goal: which means winning games, and that requires goals scored, passes completed, tackles won, saves made, training schedules, medical support and so on. In business, big goals almost always start in terms of revenue and profit. As I mentioned in an earlier chapter, there are exceptions where the owners are growing market share, looking to exit or other strategic intentions, but it is mostly about profit and revenue. So, for any department to prove their contribution, they have to start by looking at how they affect the company's profit and revenue. That means starting with a vision outside of the brand, views, leads, feeding the pipeline stereotype and looking at revenue first. We will return to this idea later in the book, but I'll leave you with one more thought to consider as we finish this chapter.

Have you ever been to a foreign country with a group of friends where only one of your party speaks the local language fluently? Who is the person your hosts most engage with? Who do all of your group want to hang around with when you go out? And who has the most influence regarding food, drink, entertainment and everything else that happens on the trip? If you want to be influential in the marketplace and the internal conversation of your organisation, you have to learn the language of both. That means understanding who your customers are beneath the data (textbook language is very different to conversational) and fluently speaking the language of the business – revenue.

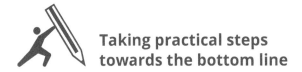

Taking practical steps towards the bottom line

In the diagram at the end of the last chapter, we showed you the differences in the way sales and marketing see things to help you open the conversation with salespeople. Discovering the following numbers and making the effort to understand how they relate to the broader commercial dynamic of the business, will create a strong foundation for conversations throughout the business. But this is not a tick-box exercise. Use the diagram below to discover who are the key influencers and decision makers in your organisation and who is best placed to arm you with this information.

The influencers behind the data

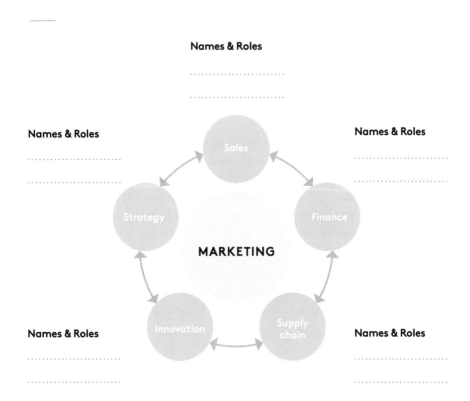

Now use your investigations to open relationships and internal networking doors for your future as a revenuist marketer. As these contacts and discussions develop, you will begin to identify opportunities for marketing to become a facilitator of joined-up conversations across these other departments with an aim to increase revenue and profit.

Trust me. Asking the right people the right questions will get yourself noticed. Try the ones below. But, be warned, they may well ask why you want to know, and you had better be ready with a commercially savvy reason. (Hint: 'a book on marketing told me to ask' is not the right answer.)

- How much did your business make in the last FY?
- What are your organisations sales targets for the next Financial Year?
- What is your sales target this Quarter?
- How does this figure differ Quarter by Quarter?
- How are your marketing budgets tied to the revenue targets for the business?

Use the space below to write a list of questions for the key 'Influencers' in your business.

Notes:

....
....
....
....
....
....
....
....
....
....
....
....
....
....

CHAPTER 9

Changing lanes: becoming a revenuist.

Who's seen those children's puzzles where you have to escape the maze or find your way to the treasure in the middle by following the pathway and avoiding the dead ends? They are based on the famous hedgerow mazes adorning historic palatial gardens or stately homes of the old British aristocracy. But in the paper versions, you simply draw your escape route with a pencil. If you are familiar with the concept, you are probably also aware of the not-so-secret fastest route to the solution. Start at the destination and work your way backwards to the start. That is hard to do in an actual maze with the high hedges blocking your view and each twist or turn designed to look exactly the same as the last, but on paper, the bird's eye view shows you precisely which route to follow.

When I look at my real-world experiences and the piece of paper in front of me, it seems almost too obvious to suggest the solution is to slam the two departments, sales and marketing, together. Equally, creating a single head of department overseeing both functions to ensure a common goal may seem oversimplistic. This is not a new idea. A quick LinkedIn search revealed 22,000 people claiming Chief Revenue Officer as a current or previous job title in the UK. I think some of the large tech firms first began to introduce the CRO role in the early 2010s, and the idea has spread further abroad to smaller organisations and across industries. I am certainly not suggesting that sales and marketing are reborn as the Revenue Department, although that is, without doubt, the primary purpose of both sides of the revenue coin. But placing one person who understands that clarity of vision as the head of both departments does make a huge amount of sense. It would be akin to starting at the exit point of the maze (or where a sale triumphantly appears at the end of a pipeline) and working back towards the big idea that kicked off the marketing campaign months or years earlier. I appreciate most people reading this book are unlikely to be able to shake up their entire internal structure and make sweeping demands of the board or human resources to that end. If you are an ambitious graduate in the first year of your marketing career, please do not barge into a meeting with your Managing Director and HR Director waving this book around claiming "Rich says..." as I doubt they will know or care who I am. You could anonymously send them a copy of the book if you like, but I promise you there are more practical things you can do yourself to affect change.

Before you jump to any other conclusions, I want to clarify that salespeople are salespeople and marketers are marketers. As we have discussed already, they typically emerge from very different moulds, often with polar opposite personalities, and there is no circumstance where they should try and be each other. But we must start to recognise that both sides of this revenue-generating coin benefit from developing the symbiotic relationship between them. As we have discussed over the last two or three chapters, one way to do that is by learning to adapt, understand, and communicate better. The other way is to unify the vision and encourage marketing departments to start with the end goal in mind – perhaps with a single Head of the Division.

Becoming a commercial influencer

I realise that not every marketer has ambitions to open the boardroom door and claim a seat, change their organisation's entire structure or direction, or even head the division. For most marketers, simply being the best they can be, earning the respect of their peers and having the carte blanche freedom to be creative is the utopian dream. Looking at the Marketer's Hierarchy of Needs model from chapter two, many brilliant marketers will be content to go from level three (having creative freedom) to level five (realising self-worth and potential), missing out level four (influence) altogether. That is fine; I understand that entirely. But the problem is, you can only achieve that, in today's commercial climate, by becoming more commercial.

On this point, Julie Fewell of Energy Marketing says, *"While the idea of the top marketing role isn't for everyone, the very nature of being a marketer means you must still want to make an impact. So effective marketers need to work with senior leaders and embed themselves within the business to ensure their activity meets its objectives. Because the only impact that matters to the role is the one that yields the maximum return to the business it is there to market".*

Marketing is a unique skill, and the marketing department still needs to exist to nurture and perfect the art of marketing, just like the sales department needs to nurture and perfect the art of sales. But both sales and marketing need to develop a better understanding of the bigger picture. For sales, it is the recognition and appreciation (and to some extent, responsibility) of the hard work, skill and time involved in bringing opportunities to their door. For marketing, it is learning to speak the language of the business – revenue and profit – more fluently.

Before I introduce you to the revenuist, let's examine the role of a CRO. This individual should come from either a sales or marketing background, but they must have a deep understanding of both, without prejudice to their own beginnings. Previous iterations or attempts at creating the CRO role have always tended to be filled by people with a strong sales background, like the Vice President of Sales and Marketing or similar titles. These positions were often the result of the sales department encircling and absorbing the marketing team within an organisation, condemning them to even more of a bullied sales admin, backroom function than before. If marketing does not step up now, I foresee the same scenario happening again, which would be a tragedy for marketing and the entire business community. For that reason, I think a strong, business-savvy marketer would make the best kind of CRO. Wherever these people emerge from, however, these are the three main characteristics they must embody:

A comprehensive understanding of their customers. Sales-people excel at uncovering customers' wants, needs, fears and desires through face-to-face conversations. They are skilled communicators and easily build relationships and trust; in some cases, they even turn commercial interactions into personal friendships where topics of discussion range far beyond work. Marketing people read customer data and spot patterns, trends and market movements better than anyone else but have less personal contact or under the skin insight. Their skill is seeing what an ideal customer is likely to want and crafting messages, images and useful information that will draw their attention to the brand in question. Wouldn't it be powerful if one joined-up department head had access to all of this skill, information and capability?

Looking beyond the product or service. As a salesperson, I find it difficult to write about this without a little bit of angst because it is such an obvious yet largely ignored concept. Instead of marketing products or services (features), marketers need to consider the intricate problems they solve for clients (benefits). This will be a significant conceptual shift for most marketing people, but it is a game-changer if you can see the importance. If you don't believe that people still get this wrong, go and look at the marketing collateral being used in your organisation today. Then give an honest assessment of how much of it is product-led, feature-heavy against real-world stories about your customers living better lives as a result of using those products.

Consider data to be your new best friend: To be a successful CRO, you have to be an expert at data analysis. This is not a contradiction of what I have said earlier about seeing beyond the data, simply a confirmation that marketing people are better suited to the role than salespeople. A CRO who truly understands customer and market data and has their finger on the pulse to accurately predict and respond to short and long term revenue goals possesses incredible power. Naturally, one of the most critical tools for CROs is their Customer Relationship Management (CRM) system because it gathers the relevant data in one place. The problem is that salespeople rarely use CRMs the way marketing need them to, and marketing tend to nag or moan about it behind their backs instead of explaining the value of using it well. (By explaining, I mean demonstrating how it will help them to close more deals.)

Appointing a knowledgeable CRO to manage both departments is the smartest thing because it is the fastest route to ensuring joined-up working and a shared vision. Aligning thinking and proving the value of collaboration by best practice, good process and open communication (including experiencing each other's roles) is guaranteed to increase revenue. But there is no point in slamming together the two departments if they act in the old ways. Both sales and marketing people need to change and become more commercial.

Paul Collier, a good friend of mine and a highly experienced B2B marketing consultant with previous roles at Dell and HP, summed it up perfectly recently. He said, *"The issue isn't the organisational chart, but the way the two departments behave: more precisely, the way they are led to behave by the way they are paid,"* and then suggested, *"you don't need to have one department if you're all measured and monitored in the same way"*.

Introducing the revenuist revolution

So, creating a CRO role would be a good start, but we have already established that not every marketer aspires to be that person and neither should they have to. But I believe every marketer who wants to survive the future shape of the commercial world needs to become a revenuist. Marketers must start to develop a strong, commercial business focus, not just a marketing one. And the irony is, that is the only way to release their creativity and allow them to become the truly remarkable, headline hitting, name-in-lights, famous marketers they are supposed to be.

Revenuists build their activities around big picture business outcomes such as revenue and margin instead of tick-box marketing tasks like producing collateral and registering conference attendees. That is what I mean by business focus: speaking the language of the boardroom (the people who control budgets and decision making) and building respect and collaborative relationships with salespeople (the people who convert marketing's hard work into revenue). When revenue and profit are the reason for the marketing campaign, it becomes evident to everyone, from the budget-setters to the deal-closers, that there will be no return on investment without the marketing activity that starts the process rolling.

I described the ideal CRO earlier in this chapter, and in the second half of the book, we will get more into the commercial attributes that marketing must embrace to survive in the new normal. So, I want to finish this chapter with a description of the revenuist marketer.

Has clarity of the business commercials: The revenuist will see ads, blogs, brochures, sign-ups, likes, shares, research, and even the grandiose dark arts of brand and digital marketing as the *means* of what they do – not the end – or the role. They recognise their role as generating relevant, targeted sales opportunities (albeit as part of a team) and have that as the crystal clear driver and purpose behind everything they do.

Manages the entire sales process: The secret to an end-to-end sales process is the CRM. Suppose marketing does claim its rightful place operating at the core of revenue generation within an organisation and gets rewarded accordingly. That means it needs to control each element of the process – from campaign to pipeline and closing the deal – or it risks losing out if sales fail to complete their part of the process. That is why the CRM system is so important. When a salesperson understands how correct use of the CRM will increase their close rates and starts inputting data and results correctly, the marketing revenuist can manage the process (including sales people's activities) and maximise its effectiveness.

Thinks big and thinks concept first: This part of a marketing-revenuist's role is only possible when the first two become foundations of their working practice. At this point, marketing can change lanes, adjust their speed and break records as freely as any salesperson. The budget is no longer the white line because the business knows that marketing is delivering a return on income. In other words, the bigger the budget, the more revenue and profit the sales and marketing divisions will generate for the business. This realisation means marketers can do what they are best at doing and what they studied so darn hard to do: marketing! Develop big picture concepts and ideas that will grab the audience's attention, engage with their emotions and needs and draw new customers to the brand. Then they can use the budget to deliver a successful brand-to-sale campaign.

If you are a marketer reading this book and think I am describing a utopian dream that could never happen in the real world, I promise you I'm not. Yes, I made up the term 'revenuist' for the purposes of this book (although I hope it appears in the real world one day), but the role most certainly exists now. That is how marketing operates in our business, in many of our client's businesses, and I increasingly hear more examples of positive change.

Are you ready to become a revenuist?

CHAPTER 10

Become greater than the sum of your superpowers.

This is the last chapter in part one of this book, and I want to use it to sum up and *really* nail home the value of working collaboratively – for everyone. In some ways, this chapter addresses a general principle for businesses: two (three, four or a team) working together is better than one person on their own. In part two, we will dig deep into the practical steps you can take to become a fully equipped marketer for today's market conditions.

Salespeople like to think of themselves as the firm's superheroes, swooping in to save the day and rescue the business with their superpower of getting customers to hand over their cash. But you do not need to watch many superhero movies to understand that when a real badass villain confronts the Hulk, Wonder Woman or even the humble Ironman, they perform better with backup. It has become a kind of movie cliché that superheroes all prefer to work alone and don't need anyone else. But with thirty minutes of the movie remaining, the obvious (to the rest of us mere mortals at least) solution is to overcome their ego and form a Super-Team.

The thing about life lessons in movies, books, anecdotes or any other media is that we all smile and agree in principle, then carry on living our lives as we were before. Trust me, ask any of my team, and they will tell you: when I believe I am right, it is tough to talk me down. I am aware of this now, and, often through gritted teeth, I force myself to listen and open the door to responding. Much of the content we have covered so far has been directed at marketing people simply because I believe they are the ones who need to instigate change. It is their livelihoods, future, and in some respects, very existence that depends on reinventing themselves. But, hitting salespeople's reaction buttons (as we have discussed) and demonstrating how marketing can help close more deals will force the good ones to react. So, this chapter is weighted a little more to salespeople and their egos.

Back in the last century, before social media, online reviews and easy access to fast, accurate, big data, most deals were closed over a Martini in a wine bar with a single decision-maker at the table. Today there is a new super-villain in town: The multi-headed procurement team. Research by Gartner found that the number of people involved in B2B purchase decisions averaged 6.8 in 2017, rising from 5.4 in 2015. I don't have access to the latest numbers, but the trend would suggest that 2021's number is well over 10.

In 2018, consultancy firm McKinsey produced a list of ways purchasing has changed over the last twenty years and suggested various approaches to make commission structures reflect the new world. Here are three of their conclusions:

MILESTONE MARKERS. We live in an increasingly instant world, where consumers can ask Alexa to buy their whim, browse the aisles of virtual stores on their doorstep, and same-day delivery is a standard. But ironically, despite the ease of click-and-collect, decisions are taking longer. Buyers scan reviews and search out the cheapest, and it seems that knowing delivery is instant means purchases often get left to the last minute. In business, this is reflected in the complexity of procurement departments, sign-off authority, audit trail, legislation, and of course, health and safety. As decision-cycles become longer and more complex, McKinsey's suggestion is to reward sales teams as prospects pass specific milestones on the way to purchase. My view is that this approach could extend before the pipeline even begins to include qualitative marketing milestones.

INPUT-RELATED COMMISSIONS. If a company operates in an omnichannel environment, where a customer may swap sales channels just before signing, it should be recognised as such. Or, if the strength of a lead stems from an existing relationship with the marketing team before it becomes a golden deal delivered into a salesperson's lap, the reward should reflect the circumstance. When any combination of a company's revenue-generating functions closes sales, the team who do most of the work should accrue the lion's share of the commissions. That might not be the traditional format, but it does sound fair, right?

CROSS-REGION RECOGNITION. We live in an era of global, matrixed organisations where teams working together on deals can be the deciding factor in reaching a win. In these instances, cooperation should be encouraged by giving both teams 100% credit for the result. Arrangements like this would also act as a positive precursor introducing cooperative work into the company culture.

The McKinsey report got me thinking about another change in buying behaviour relative to the marketing theme we are discussing here. Buyers, particularly in B2B environments, tend to rely on their own research and the opinions of influencers and analysts before speaking to salespeople. In many cases, the cold hard truth is that buyers are well over halfway to their decision before even talking to someone who can take their order. So, where marketing departments have performed famously and generated a quality lead who needs little more than hand-holding across the line, of course, they should be rewarded. To think any different is so utterly small-minded as to be anti-sales in every way, shape or form.

I can imagine salespeople reading the list above now and thinking about having to share their commission. There is no way a suggestion like that will go down well in the sales department. The truth is: a percentage of any salesperson's deals are hard-fought battles where they deserve every scrap of reward and probably more besides, but... there will also be the tap-ins where they do little more than show up and smile. The salesperson needs to understand (and I hope I have demonstrated the point so far in this book) that cooperative working will increase the number of tap-ins. The result may mean sharing some of their commission or reward with other contributors to the sale, but there will be more sales. In other words, everyone wins more often, and there is more of the win to share around the team.

Euphoric highs and damning lows will still live at the beating heart of the sales department. This must remain because that environment charges a salesperson's nature and keeps them hungry for success. I am not suggesting we reduce sales to a spreadsheet process where the wild celebrations of closing a deal become tick-boxes and multi-coloured bar charts. Salespeople's focus must remain on the lucrative target and the thrill of the chase; otherwise, they will not survive the inevitable lows and daily rejections I shared with you earlier. My experience is that the team element of working alongside marketing colleagues, as valued partners focused on delivering sales results, helps keep the momentum regardless of the inevitable emotional swings.

Lead generation is a function of sales

Rupert Bedell, the Vice President of B2B Marketing at American Express, has absolute clarity on the benefits and rewards of sales and marketing truly working together. He describes his role within Amex as B2B marketing across EMEA (from TV advertising at the top of the funnel through to member referrals and everything in between), covering 14 markets, with the UK as the biggest. Interestingly, he defines the activity of lead generation as anything that results in a sale.

"In most organisations," Rupert says, *"you might have a brand team, a campaign management function, another team working on lead generation, and one providing sales support or working in some field support capacity. And it's rare for them to be in complete harmony with*

each other. At American Express, we've worked hard to tie these goals together as upper-funnel and lower-funnel marketing: brand message at the top and lead generation in a lower funnel. You can't plan for either in the absence of the other, and over-focus on lead generation risks losing awareness and consideration of our products in the market at the top end". Rupert explains, *"Of course, everyone knows Amex, but a lot of small businesses in the UK, assume we are expensive and elite, so we've worked hard to become a relevant partner, with relevant propositions for small businesses. And proof that the brand message works is evidenced by the harmony between the two and the lead generation delivering results".*

So, even within marketing teams in large organisations, there are elements of siloed working resulting in operational and performance inefficiencies. And where that happens, it needs to be addressed before seeking to fix any directional differences with the sales team. One of the other interesting things I learned from Rupert Bedell when we interviewed him for *The CMO Show* podcast in May 2021 is that Amex's marketing department has a commercial scorecard. The company recognises that marketing is a core strength that underpins the entire business. Without those two elements of marketing working seamlessly together, upper-funnel messaging, designed to attract the specifically targeted market and lower-funnel, proactively turning attention into leads (or online conversions) for the sales team, the business fails. They do not measure the number of social media views and likes, how many posts go out, or the internal response to the latest advert. It is all about the contribution to the bottom line and the number of sales that marketing generates or help to set up for sales to do their thing.

Rupert said, *"Some marketers are more commercial than others, good on the sales and finance numbers and very target driven, and some aren't. But you have to bring everybody on the journey to a point where they all know what the plan is and are comfortable with their contribution to it. Everyone needs to know how the team is performing (daily, weekly, monthly) and understand there is a goal, and we are 20%, 10% or 5% off. The entire unit starts to move more cohesively. The brand and messaging team starting to work in unison with the lead generation team because if* one or other fails their job, we all fail the scorecard". What I liked most in all Rupert's comments was when he said, *"I wouldn't want to work in a marketing organisation where you didn't have very clear commercial pressure over brand metrics. I actually think it is harder to be successful in a marketing organisation with no clear commercial KPIs to tell you how you are contributing to the team effort".*

Back in the late 1800s, US Postmaster General John Wanamaker, known as one of the pioneers of marketing, famously said, *"Half the money I spend on advertising is wasted: the trouble is I don't know which half".* Today, there is literally no excuse for not knowing what works and what doesn't. We live in the age of data and metrics. Marketers can measure everything, and a good CRM system (providing salespeople buy-in to the value of using it properly) should be able to tell you the value delivered by each marketing activity and the contribution it makes to the bottom line.

Our job, as marketers, is to fully embrace the principle, recognise that we hold the most influential hand, play our cards boldly and intelligently, and build a team of superheroes.

PART TWO

Establishing the new marketing identity.

CHAPTER 11

Where did marketing start to slide?

In the first part of this book, the primary focus was the relationship between sales and marketing. We looked at each department's unique strengths and inherent weaknesses, and I hope I have convinced you these opposite sides of the same valuable coin need each other more than ever. I will refer back to this partnership in this second part of the book, but our main focus will be the need for marketing to become more commercial – and how to achieve that end.

To understand where marketing is today, we first need to look at how it got here. And to see where marketing needs to go, we must explore some of the glory days of its past. So, part two is all about becoming the marketer of the future – today.

Twenty years ago, there were probably five specific marketing roles; now, there are closer to fifty. Today you could be a researcher, executive, product manager, buyer, PPC specialist, copywriter, social media manager, content manager, SEO specialist, promotions planner, media planner, brand manager, art director, digital marketer, communications manager, email marketer, growth marketer, graphic designer, website developer, analyst; or dozens of other things. (These are actual job titles I found advertised online.) Now, all of these marketing elements may exist in one form or another, and perhaps the best way for a company to achieve that end is to create a specialist role for each. But this approach is central to the problem for modern marketing.

Imagine trying to write a sentence with nothing more than the vowels at your disposal. Or maybe you are restricted to the letters on the middle row of your qwerty keyboard. I doubt you could construct any meaningful communication with those restrictions. The fact is that any single letter, or even a sub-set of letters set aside for a specialist purpose, is not the alphabet. To communicate coherently, with the freedom to express both awe and pizazz, you need access to all the letters. By definition, the alphabet is a standardised set of basic written symbols or graphemes that represent the phonemes of certain spoken languages (thank you Wikipedia).

Digital Marketing is not marketing. Search Engine Optimisation is not marketing. Social Media is not marketing. And I am very well aware I might risk contradicting some big reputation names with this one: content is not marketing either. These are all essential cogs in the modern marketing alphabet, and perhaps content *is* king (although I prefer to think of it as the oil that keeps the machine working), but they are no more marketing than Y, O, and U are the alphabet. And the problem with employing someone as a specialist and telling that person they are a marketer is that they misunderstand the role of marketing: to spell out coherent sentences that lead to sales and revenue. This purpose has been lost, and as the roles within marketing increased from five to fifty, the true definition became diluted.

What is marketing?

The American Marketing Association defines marketing as 'The performance of business activities that direct the flow of goods and services from producer to consumer or user'.

Richard Still and Edward Cundiff, authors of the best-selling Essentials of Marketing, use the definition 'The term used to describe collectively those business functions most directly concerned with the demand stimulating and demand fulfilling activities of the business enterprise'.

Philip Kotler, regarded by many as The Father of Modern Marketing, says, 'Marketing is a social and managerial process by which individuals and groups obtain what they need and want by creating and exchanging products and value with each other'. Kolter also said, 'Marketing is meeting the needs of your customer at a profit'. This is one of my favourite definitions because of its simplicity and directness.

Similarly, the Chartered Institute of Marketing published this definition in 2017 'Marketing is the management process responsible for identifying, anticipating and satisfying customer requirements profitably'.

Far be it for me to challenge these experts or established institutions, but these statements highlight two things. Firstly, a universally agreed definition of marketing does not seem to exist, and secondly, it is *definitely* not SEO, digital or social media. I even searched (and searched) for a conclusive description from Mark Ritson and could not find anything watertight to share with you.

If you thought all of that was a build-up to Richard Hadler's definition of marketing, I am sorry to disappoint you; that is not what this book is about either. The next chapter will examine the closest concept to a foundation principle of what defines marketing as I can think of – but with an important additional element. Before we arrive there, I want to get back to understanding what went wrong to take marketing's eyes so far off the ball.

From the year dot until now

As discussed, there is a clear distinction between media and marketing (or the plethora of methods for attracting customers and the greater ideals of how and why). Advertising has been around since the days of tribal exchanges, bartering goods for services and swapping shiny objects in exchange for food and clothing in makeshift marketplaces. Civilisations from Summaria to the Egyptians and the Babylonians to the Romans record promotional activities to sell merchandise and services. Maker's marks have been identified on pottery pieces in India and other countries, dating back over 3000 years. It is hard to know if any bigger picture, corporate strategy or ten-year exit plan lay behind any of these ancient attempts to sell more products, or if it was a case of trial, error and then employ the strategy that seemed to create the most sales.

Over the last two centuries, as print became cheaper, more accessible and diversified in substrate and size, advertising reached its heyday. By the late 1800s, posters lined so many London walls they were eventually banned and replaced by rented billboard space. Manufacturers produced leaflets by the thousands and gave birth to the junk mail industry (often referred to as spam thanks to an obscure Monty Python reference). Within a few decades of the 1920s, radio advertising emerged. It wasn't long after the invention of television that the toothpaste firm Gibbs launched one of the first TV advertising campaigns. Over the years that followed, as each new technology and medium emerged, companies jumped on the various bandwagons to fight for the consumer's attention. And, as the digital age accelerated into our living rooms, bedrooms, kitchens, cars, laptops, phones, tablets and everything else, the noise has become deafening.

And it is that cacophony of sounds, all desperately trying to outsell, talk over, keep pace with, imitate, replicate, shout louder, befriend, entertain, entice, include and barrage with more content than the competition, that brings us to the modern state of affairs. Perhaps an accurate definition of what marketing is (as opposed to what it should be) could simply be 'noise'.

In 1957, the President of the American Marketing Association, Wroe Alderson, published a book called Marketing Behavior and Executive Action, which many people view as a seminal work about the science and psychology of marketing strategy. In the decades leading up to and following this, people like Henry Ford, Ray Kroc (the man behind MacDonalds), Walt Disney and David Ogilvy demonstrated the power of building a brand over the cost of posting an advert. And many more big thinkers began evaluating, strategising and striving to understand what it meant to market products and services scientifically and profitably to people who actually wanted them. Other textbooks and studies on sales and marketing psychology were written, and the art became a feature of business schools and formal education. But one thing never changed: the emphasis was always on using creative ways to harness the science of consumer behaviour and encourage people to buy more stuff.

However, I believe that focus has now changed. The change was so slow and subtle, yet surrounded by the mega-fast speed and excitement of the online revolution of the 1990s, most people barely noticed. Instead of the clear goal of directing more legitimate buyers to the till or the salesperson's door, the emphasis shifted to activities, output and making noise. Please carefully consider the conclusion in that last sentence because I promise you there is a difference between the two states of play.

What does truly great marketing look like?

In 1964, with the dark emotions of World War Two still lingering in the hearts of many around the UK, Europe and the USA, Volkswagon decided they needed a big idea to remove the prejudice or nationalistic attitudes. To add fire to any conscious or unconscious bias lingering within their biggest markets, the VW Beetle, in particular, had notorious associations reaching to the top of the Nazi movement. So, in a bold move, they employed an agency to develop a campaign to warm the cold shoulder and refocus consumers on the benefits of their car.

The black and white (for younger readers, that is what TV was then) advert they designed starts with the camera focused on the front wheels of a vehicle driving through the snow across a dark, unwelcoming backdrop. Gradually a car comes into view through the cloudy mist and passes trees and hedgerows on a surface barely recognisable as a road. The only sound is the crunch of the tyres on the hardened snow as the car trudges on regardless. Thirty seconds into the scene, a voice slowly says, "Have you ever wondered what the man who drives the snowplough drives to the snowplough?" The advert ends with the Beetle parking outside a large shed and the snowplough emerging to clear the roads so all the lesser car users can get to work. The scene takes little more than a minute, but its legacy has lasted half a century already.

If you search for 'VW beetle snowplough commercial', you can watch the advert for yourself (and apologies for spoiling the punchline). What they achieved with the commercial is brilliant on several levels, but the main one was how it promoted one simple big idea: this car is fabulously reliable!

A more modern example of creative storytelling to sell a powerful idea was a 2016 advert from the 124-year-old, 300,000-employee, heavy manufacturing and engineering B2B behemoth, GE. As part of its Unimpossible Missions series, the scene starts in a bleak, mountainous area where scientists collect a snowball and secure it in a high-tech cold box. They transport it by an escort of 4WDs over rocky terrain to a foundry, with the gravelly-voiced narrator explaining how they are about to embark on an almost impossible mission, citing how it has a snowball's chance in hell of success. Stressing the scientific conditions under which the experiment is taking place and retaining an air of extreme jeopardy, the frames flash from scientists in labcoats to heavy machinery and molten metal, as the gritty commentary describes what is about to happen. GE's brightest minds had developed a specialist container and hoped it would preserve the acquired snowball as it descended into a lake of hellish fire at over 2000 degrees.

The roar of approval as the snowball emerged, still frozen, tells you that 'hope' was an apt description of the scientists' expectations. The three-minute story was big and bold, intriguing and impossible to ignore, and I can promise you there was no discussion about budget when they conceived the idea. It was an atmospheric and beautifully shot piece of cinema, but the caption at the end, 'imagine what other impossible things we can do', was the real story.

As with the VW advert, I suggest you search for 'GE snowball's chance in hell' and see what great marketing looks like today. We will unpick this example in a bit more depth in chapter fourteen.

Please understand me here; I'm not a modern marketer who gets nostalgic and gooey-eyed over stories of the marketing heydays of yesteryear and has lost sight of the real world. I realise the world has moved on, technology has changed everything, and marketing has evolved from two or three channels to twenty or thirty. I'm not suggesting we ditch the internet. But I think we can simplify things into two clear activities that hang off the one big idea. I am talking about brand activation and sales activation.

Creative clarity beats an abundance of noise

In principle, this has changed very little from the early days of marketing, even if the media options have increased considerably. In short, it is about articulating the brand, coming up with a creative narrative and being different. The channels were face-to-face, printed media and some out-of-home advertisements. And because there were fewer routes to consumers' ears, and every brand was fighting over the same audience in the same places, the focus had to be on creativity. So, you had Mum, Dad, a 7-year-old boy, his 10-year-old sister and a moody teenager all watching the same Saturday night TV show in one room. Can you imagine such a time even existed? And each member of that family knew that happiness was a cigar called Hamlet, Milky Bars turned even the smallest kids into the coolest cowboy, and you needed Shake n' Vac to put the freshness back. It wasn't rocket science, but the messages stuck.

To some degree, that was all marketing needed to do at that time... or pretty much all it could do. A degree of sales activation (clever aisle placement in stores, for example) was possible, but the opportunities were limited. Today there are dozens, even hundreds, of ways to communicate messages to an audience and even more methods to engage a sale. The possibilities for sales activation and brand activation are now endless. This should be good news for the marketer, but what it has done is place the focus on covering the bases instead of creating the big idea. Marketing today has become a cacophony of noise over a precise solo or harmonic duet sung in perfect clarity. And, worse, each instrument is often out of time or tune with others in the band.

That, in a nutshell, is why marketers today feel compelled to complicate everything they do and believe: even messing around with fundamental principles that were discovered (not created, and there is a difference) through observation and study over decades. The Four Ps have been redefined as Seven Ps, and there are now eight or nine Cs of marketing. I have found a list of the 77 essential marketing tools, and you can get degrees in social media management, digital marketing, and pretty much any of the other 25, 52 or 93 versions of the role that now exists. Marketing education is as confusing today as most marketing communication.

So, at the risk of contradicting myself completely, let's move into the next chapter and have a look at the Fifth P. The one that will help us get back to using the original four properly.

CHAPTER 12

The four Ps means peanuts! What about profit?

The principle of the Four Ps should form the foundation stone of every marketer's education. It is the bread and butter of the profession, and I would lose all credibility if (as a self-confessed, hard-nosed, ex-salesperson) I was to launch an attack on such a fundamental truth. But, from the first time I heard the principle, it always bugged me that there was no mention of profit. So let me be clear here. I do not want to mess with the underlying, immovable and 100% reliable certainty underpinning the Four Ps. Since Jerry McCarthy first published the idea in his 1960 book, Basic Marketing - A Managerial Approach, it became the model from which almost everything else grew. And I, for one, still believe it is a failsafe, and all efforts to adapt and upgrade it are similar symptoms of modern marketing's tendency to over-complicate, like those I described in the last chapter.

The reason I want to draw attention to profit is not to change or add to the tried and tested formula but to refocus on the purpose of using such a valuable tool. One of the great ironies of creativity is that a framework can maximise its effectiveness by translating an inspired idea into a practical one. That is what the Four Ps were designed to achieve and what they should still be used for today – to generate a result. The problem is that the confused state of modern marketing has caused marketers to forget why they are doing the job in the first place. Namely, to proactively drive and support the generation of revenue and profit.

McCarthy explained that the original principle describes the four elements of the marketing mix a marketer must consider and understand when translating their idea into a customer message. So, for those non-marketing readers, here is a simple overview of the Four Ps.

PRODUCT. The marketer must be involved in the design, product development, functionality, packaging, range, maintenance, and guarantees for their products or services. There is no point in selling something that the customers do not want or need, so it is a critical element of marketing's role to listen to their prospect and client base and adapt their products and services accordingly. From my time as a salesperson, I rarely sold an off-the-shelf solution. Almost everything I ever exchanged for revenue resulted from questioning, listening, and responding to my conversations with the marketplace. (Again, this is why building that relationship with the sales team is so critical for marketers.)

PRICE. This is as much a part of marketing as the brand, the clever one-liner and the PPC ad. The marketer needs to decide if their market is volume with a low price or niche with a high price; is it a premium product where the price is part of the quality message? Or for a budget audience where five pence less than one hundred pounds will make all the difference. Discounts, bundling, special offers and credit terms are as relevant to the marketing process and strategy as the headline and the colour scheme.

PLACE. To maintain the 'P' headline, this element of the marketing mix stands for the place where the products and services are delivered to the customer. McCarthy originally described this as distribution or logistics but allowed himself a little 'fudge' to add symmetry to his alliterative formula. The term refers to how the services are implemented for a customer or the products arrive: through shops, e-commerce, delivery, collection or download.

PROMOTION. The final P is perhaps what most people outside of marketing would describe as marketing. That is because it is how marketing manifests itself, through adverts, social media, product placement, branding, PR, and all the other forms of content companies use across today's abundance of media channels. The two levels of marketing we have discussed earlier in the book, brand activation and sales activation, form parts of the promotion area of the marketing mix.

It is worth noting that modern marketers tend to talk about the Four Ps in terms of their Four Cs equivalents. There is clearly some thinking behind this repackaging exercise, and I don't particularly want to discuss the wrongs and rights of the change. But I know many astute marketers who believe, as I do, that the P to C switch has caused more harm than good. Before I address the problem it has created, let me explain how Four Ps became Four Cs in a seamless and alliterative transition that only a marketing mind could muster. And I would like to thank my good friend, Louis Fernandes, for his help to describe what, how and why the Four Cs have created an issue throughout marketing.

The idea with the Four Cs approach is its focus on the modern niche approach to marketing (made possible by technology) and away from the more generalist approach of the past decades.

CUSTOMER (replaces product). There is some logic in customer (or consumer) replacing product because it is important to understand what the market needs rather than what companies want to sell them. So focus on the market is the correct approach. But if you revisit my previous explanation of the product (P), you will recognise that developing products to meet customer needs was always central to the purpose. Marketing absolutely should be involved in product development because marketers should understand what their customers need.

COST (replaces price). Perhaps there is a good reason to think about cost rather than price because it does suggest a broader understanding of what is required to create a profit. But I also believe that a comprehensive insight into why marketing should be involved in pricing decisions was sufficient for recognising this requirement. You cannot intelligently set a price for any product or service simply by deciding what it should be. As explained in my earlier price description, that decision must consider the delivery cost, the margin you want to make, and the market you are trying to sell to (budget or premium).

CONVENIENCE (replaces place). This change is (somewhat) relevant in modern marketing terms because convenience is a bigger factor than ever before for consumers. But, as with the other 'P' terms, a complete understanding of the original place description (or, as explained, distribution) demonstrates that the original word made the point perfectly.

COMMUNICATION (replaces promotion). Of all the C to P transitions in the modernisation of this formula, this is the one that actually causes a problem. The others have some justification, but on the face of it seems to me to be change for change's sake. However, it appears to have spawned an idea that has spread like a virus throughout marketing departments everywhere. Supported by other intelligent sounding modern sayings like 'content is king', people have bought into the idea that producing lots of good quality content will solve any company's marketing dilemma. I challenge you to ask around the marketing department in your business, and I reckon nine out of ten marketers will agree that content is the principle, most important thing. It isn't!

The idea that 'content is king' (in isolation) is countered by the much older and far truer saying, 'If you don't know where you are going, all roads will take you there'. You absolutely must have a clear vision of the big idea first. Promotion is a far better description of the activity because it makes you think about what you are trying to communicate, not just the volume and amount of message.

So, as Louis explained this to me, it demonstrated how this focus on content delivery, above everything else, has increasingly put all the emphasis in most marketing departments on sales activation with little or no attention on the big idea (or activating the brand). This approach focuses on the short-term, quick wins at the expense of the bigger picture proposition. Les Binet and Peter Field's brilliant 2013 book, The Long and the Short of it, comprehensively proves that this approach does not work.

As a result, many marketers (not all of them if you are reading this and taking offence) have come to see their role as little more than communication and content generation, with a heavy emphasis on communicating across digital channels. Digital marketing is simply a modern facet of the promotion function described by Jerry McCarthy's Four Ps principle over seventy years ago – before digital was even a thing. Digital marketing is just marketing. And any marketer who identifies themselves as a digital marketer would do well to educate themselves in what marketing is really there to achieve.

My long introduction to this chapter's heading, 'What about profit?', has landed us at a challenge to digital marketing and digital marketers. That was not my specific purpose; it is simply the case that digital marketing represents the clearest symptom of modern marketing's problem (but it is not the only one). So I will offer an apology to digital marketers if any are still offended. The point does, however, bring me definitively to my reason for writing this chapter. If we can return to an understanding that marketing's bottom line purpose is to drive revenue, sales and profit, we find ourselves in a place where we can also address the bigger picture.

Revenue, not content, solves everything

I will caveat here a point made earlier in the book that not every organisation's headline strategy is the generation of revenue and profit.

You will need to be clear on what the board and shareholders of your organisation are looking to achieve and use that as the fundamental driver for your marketing strategy. And substitute that objective for my reference to profit in the rest of this chapter.

The bottom line is: marketing is about moving the needle and taking an organisation nearer to its targets and objectives. It is not content that solves everything; it is profitable revenue or sales. And when you are clear on this point, it releases your freedom to be creative and build a brand (trust, desire, confidence) that customers want to buy from. Looking at the end goal compels you to embrace the entire marketing mix: do we have a product that customers trust and need? If not, can we adapt to make it fit – or do we have to create a new version? Is our product or service appropriately priced to support our positioning, attract the right customers, and generate the profit the board is looking to achieve? What do we need to do to make the place where our products and services are sold to our customers more accessible, inviting and appropriate to the market? If it isn't working, how can we reimagine the distribution of what we do? Then, with all of these questions answered and an understanding of the parameters and profitability we are aiming for, we can let our creativity get to work and design the big idea to promote the brand and turn our message into profit.

In the next chapter, we will cover some of the most exciting content in this book, looking at the concept of losing the budget and the sense of ticking boxes. That is what success does for you. When you achieve what your employers want you to achieve, the smart ones will let you keep on doing it. Why would they question success? In most businesses, things operate better if the company is making money and profit. When an organisation is profitable, the board can invest in its people, systems, infrastructure, training, product development, marketing, working environment and technology. Profitable companies (the ones run by people worth working for) recognise where their good fortune comes from and encourage those departments to keep being amazing. No one questions the superstar. That's why understanding and focusing on the end goal is so much more important than writing a blog post.

CHAPTER 13

Escape the bounds
of the budget.

This chapter is really about establishing your right to be creative. Previously, I talked about the need to start with the big idea and think about the ultimate goal of marketing: to generate genuine sales opportunities.

So, what would happen in marketing departments around the country if the budget came down from head office at the beginning of the year and it simply said, 'There is no budget – go and generate a return on investment'? And in the small print, the message reads, 'We do not care how many blog posts you write, sign-ups you get at the roadshow, likes you amass on our social media pages, names you add to the email list or leads you pass to the sales team. We simply want you to contribute to top line revenue or bottom line profit targets we have set for the next two years'. How would you, as a marketing professional, handle that momentous memo?

If you think I am talking nonsense, I promise you I am not. I might have waxed lyrical describing the wording of the instruction coming down from on high, but there are smart-thinking companies out there who operate along these lines. And they do it because they know their marketing departments have clarity on their purpose and the organisation's ambitions, and they have learned to trust their judgement about the best way to achieve that result. So, if you are reading this and thinking, no way could ever happen here, I urge you to try utilising some of the ideas in this book to prove your case, or I would refer you back to the move-on arrow in the Marketer's Hierarchy of Needs model.

The irony is that you would still have to use some level of measurement to prove your efforts are working. For one thing, you would have to know the revenue target and how much your efforts need to generate. And while knowing the number and tracking your contribution are essential, neither of these is the best place to start. Just imagine getting all of the creative minds in your team together and asking questions like, who is our customer, what do they actually want, where are they getting that now, how can we do better, what messages would resonate with their emotions, and what do we need to do to grab their attention and compel them to love us and trust us? Wouldn't that be a wonderful, empowering and worthwhile way to start a campaign? Isn't that what you signed up for?

In our business, this is how we approach every single project. We dig beneath our customers' skin to discover their purpose, ambitions, identity, and USPs; and strive to understand their customers and prospects' wants and needs. Then we help them develop big picture ideas and concepts that will actually resonate with that audience. With that freedom of thought as the backdrop, we encourage creativity, leftfield imaginations, thinking completely differently and engaging 'no holds barred' vision. It is like skiing off-piste, driving a broad highway without lane restrictions or skydiving for the first time. Yes, it can be a little uncomfortable, even scary, especially for customers working with us for the first time, but boy, what a thrill to see those ideas emerge, expand, bloom and then land safely and take shape.

The creative concept should always come first and foremost in the project. And it is after we have discovered the big idea, and only then, that we begin to think about how to execute the plan – with a budget in mind. In Stephen R. Covey's famous book, The 7 Habits of Highly Effective People, he describes the story of two woodcutters chopping down trees and how one spends the first hour sharpening his saw while the other dives straight into chopping. If you haven't read the book (spoiler alert), the one with the sharpened saw ends the day having cut down significantly more trees with less effort. Covey uses the anecdote to press home the productivity impact of effective planning, but the principle is applicable in this context too. You will be amazed at how much easier and more efficient it is to build a campaign and allocate the activities needed to amplify an idea when you are clear on the concept. And you'll also be surprised at just how far the budget stretches when you know what the vision looks like before you start to build it.

Ditch the marketing plan

Chapter fourteen will present a comprehensive model we teach our customers about leading with the creative concept. We call it Bravery in B2B Marketing because we understand that it takes guts to change lanes, as described above. I am sure you will enjoy working through the content, and I hope you feel inspired by it. But for the rest of this chapter, I want to get back to escaping the bounds of the budget.

A marketing plan is not the answer! How can you create a plan to achieve anything unless you know what it looks like in the first place? Remember the maze puzzle I referred to in chapter nine? It is the same idea here. You have to start with the entire vision in mind so you know how to reverse engineer your route to the treasure. Although marketers are hot on data analysis and CRM, they are not administrators, schedulers or digital technicians – they are creative people who can summon ideas and vision. And when that creativity has the licence to flourish, it becomes the golden ticket in assisting accelerated business growth. Marketers who think creatively and live outside of the box have the most significant impact on sales performance and profit because their work turns heads internally and externally. Any other approach to marketing reduces its function to little more than a cog in the wheel.

My vision of outstanding marketing is when a salesperson turns up to a meeting for the first time, and the prospect says, I asked to see you because that advert about time-travel being a genuine possibility has got the whole office talking. Or the telesales team reports target busting levels of inbound calls – all wanting to know more about the astonishing new colour the technical team have invented. That is what I mean about having an impact internally and externally – when creativity is leading the way, marketing becomes impossible to ignore! No marketing plan on earth can compete with a killer, creative, leftfield idea.

Be different!

If ever there was an overused, and quite frankly misused, phrase in marketing, it is 'we need to be different'. I agree with the sentiment, but people interpret that as coming up with a version of what everyone else is doing. They claim 'different' then set about rewriting competitor's blogs in different words; reusing the same (old) video content on the latest social media platform; rebranding just because it's 'been a few years', or trying to create a version of the John Lewis advert. Different isn't five car manufacturers all having a car identical to a Volkswagon with a different badge or buying a white-label app and adding your logo. Different is Steve Job's market-shifting iPhone launch in 2007 and Elon Musk's first Tesla rolling off the production line.

When I started with Raconteur, I became their highest revenue generator in my first year as a salesperson. I continued to outperform everyone else *and* my previous targets throughout my time in that role. But here is the thing: around 80% of the solutions I sold didn't even exist until I negotiated the deal with the client and our internal team. And here is the even bigger lesson. This all happened before I had my epiphany about the importance of marketing. And I genuinely believe that if I had utilised my marketing team correctly during that time and had realised they are far more creative and innovative than I could be (by the very fact that they are marketers), I could have doubled my outcomes. More fool me – but at least I know better now and have this opportunity to help others avoid doing the same.

Get some skin in the game

Salespeople are stretched by targets, while budgets restrict marketing departments. In many ways, those are the polar opposites of each other. And yet, as I have probably laboured the point enough, they are also two sides of an equal coin and aim for the same target. But salespeople are the ones out there taking risks, ducking and diving, changing lanes, pushing the needle and surviving only by the success of their achievements. Please excuse the generalisation (I know this is not the same everywhere), but marketing departments do not tend to be such dynamic, risk-taking, live or die by your results type environments. So, if ditching the marketing plan appeals to you, and you are eager to live up to your creativity – you might have to live by the seat of your pants too.

It's time for marketing to have skin in the game. If marketers are to escape the bounds of the budget and let their creativity lead their output, they need to prove their work is making an impact. And that means there should be a reward, like salespeople receive, to recognise their contribution to closing more deals. I'm not suggesting for a minute that marketers do not already work hard. Trust me, I know about all-nighters before a big customer event and being asked to rewrite the plan at the last moment on the whim of the CEO. What I am referring to are risk and reward. Asking for the right to be creative, coming up with some innovative, out-of-the-box, inspired ideas, then delivering a measurable result. If you are going to do marketing right, you have to be able to prove it worked. And if you can do that year-in-year-out, you will never be confronted with a budget again, and your reward will be worth more than just a pat on the back.

Imagine getting a bonus based on company revenue, (or in other words, what the sales team generated based on the marketing team's work). Recently, at a Raconteur hosted roundtable event, when one senior marketer said they got paid like this, they got bombarded with questions. For example, someone asked, "Doesn't that mean you lose your bonus if sales mess up?" That is old-style, sales versus marketing thinking, right there. The marketer's response was simple and empowering, "I've made it part of my role to ensure they don't". The discussion went in various directions, but in essence, it came down to the marketer taking responsibility for seeing their good work used the way they intended. The CRM monitored how sales were progressing leads through the funnel and reported the information to marketing. In turn, the sales team came to enjoy marketing proactively feeding them relevant collateral, guidance and offering help to keep the sale on track. And this combined focus on a common target was reaping significant rewards and smashing targets.

What also emerged from that conversation was the realisation that you can encourage change as much as you like, but both sides must have skin in the game to make it happen. This means two things. Firstly, marketers should be responsible for, and be measured against, seeing the deal through to completion. Not just handing over leads and hoping it will go somewhere. Secondly, sales and marketing should have the same rewards and incentives. I don't mean those half-baked attempts to incentivise marketing by creating a complex commission bonus with an, at best, tentative link to business outcomes that only the Financial Director understands. I mean clear, equal and comparable, success-related metrics that hold sales and marketing accountable to the same objectives and rewards. The business benefits will soon follow if you can get these natural teammates working together to achieve the same results. Before you know it, stressful bottlenecks like lead-handover become a thing of the past, cross-company unity replaces playground tittle-tattle and rivalry, and revenue will increase significantly.

Of course, all this relies on buy-in from sales. Initially, there may be some misunderstanding or even hostility that marketing is suddenly poking their long noses into 'sales' stuff, and sales are losing credit for closing deals. But, if you can use some of the ideas and understanding I have suggested earlier in this book, I know you can help them understand how a stronger revenue line means more credit (financial and non-financial) to share around.

Again, I know that you might not be in a position to create these sorts of sweeping changes in the culture and organisation of your business. But you could leave a copy of this book in the boardroom, send it to the directors or be more purple and make your contribution impossible to ignore. How about writing up your proposal in a single plan, proving the impact of starting with a creative idea and working it through to the ka-ching?

CHAPTER 14

Be as good as you think you are.

In this chapter, we will work through one of the creativity models we teach our alan. clients. There are two reasons for including this exercise in the book. Firstly, I hope I have inspired marketers to be more confident about their positioning within their organisations, and I believe these principles can help promote that even further. Secondly, having reached the position where marketing departments can cast off the budget burden and start being creative, I want to encourage them to be brave in that creativity. Thinking *differently* does not mean a different version of something someone else has done. Thinking *ahead* does not mean looking for and jumping on the current bandwagon. Think adventurously, don't create just a bigger version of someone else's big idea. And think for yourself. By definition, the majority are average (think about that a moment), so don't be overly influenced by what your competition does. Be brave and get creative!

For the sake of credibility, I have already made it quite clear that I am a salesperson at heart, not a natural marketer. So you may not be surprised that much of this chapter has been influenced by the brilliance of our Creative Director, Benedict Buckland.

Most marketing is boring, expected and repetitive

Before any marketers get all defensive and upset with the headline above, that is not purely my opinion. A 2020 research project from our sister company, Raconteur, found that 71% of B2B marketers working in large organisations in London believed most marketing to be boring, expected and repetitive.

In chapter eleven, I put forward one of GE's Unimpossible Mission adverts to exemplify outstanding, creative modern B2B marketing. I am sure most marketers will agree with its merits and attention-grabbing message, while others might have agreed with my assessment through Emperor's New Clothes Syndrome. There may be a few who are honest enough to say they didn't really get the point. Let me explain why that might be.

GE is one of the largest companies in the world, with an incredible history that has left an indelible mark on many aspects of all our lives. You will certainly know the name, even if you're not aware of what the company does. Its website's 'about us' page says the following:

"No other American company can claim a heritage of innovation as deep and broad as GE. From Thomas Alva Edison's first incandescent light bulb to the latest jet engine brimming with internet-connected sensors and 3D-printed parts, GE has pioneered technologies that have spurred world-transforming changes and improved the lives of billions. We've encapsulated GE's global impact in nine different industries, highlighting four key technological transformations where we have consistently led the way. Together, these moments trace an arc of innovation that has no parallel—a proven 150-year commitment to progress that will help propel a brighter future for the world."

Its customers (or ideal audience for this particular campaign) are scientists or technologists, and the reason this advert might not have appealed to everyone is that it was designed to compel these people to stop and watch. I think it creates an irresistible sense of adventure, jeopardy and need-to-know suspense for most people, but it wasn't aimed at me, and probably not at you either. That is an important point to remember as we investigate why it works, where the idea came from, how it was developed and, most importantly, how it represents a practical framework for bravery in modern marketing.

One last point, before we start. I know there will be readers who are thinking, that is all well and good, but we don't have a budget for something like that. Organisations like GE and John Lewis might be equipped to create a mini-movie series to generate interest in their story and start a conversation, but my budget doesn't stretch to cinema. I get that, but please remember the previous chapter; this is not about the budget; it promotes a creativity-first approach; we will come to the budget later.

The five steps to bravery in B2B creativity

STEP ONE. *Determine your DNA.* Somewhere in every large organisation, there will be a mission statement or a set of foundational principles and beliefs that are supposed to represent what the business is all about. The problem is that most people employed by that organisation have not looked at that statement since their induction week and have no idea why they are there. Within the marketing team, I suspect the awareness of that 'why' might be heightened, but it doesn't always translate into the core message of any campaign. So, I would encourage you to gain absolute clarity about the DNA of the business before starting any campaign. Relaying or revisiting this cornerstone of the organisation might be the first bold step your marketing team needs to employ.

You discover your DNA by asking questions like:

- Why does the company exist?
- What is our USP?
- What difference do we make in the world or to our customers?
- What are our key brand messages or characteristics?

This is an in-depth exercise and would take more than a chapter in a book to explore in full. As an example of the conclusion a company should reach, GE's core values are represented through Innovation, Technology and Progress. They say: *"innovation, technology and progress have been in our DNA for 124 years, and we try hard to reach both core and new audiences in ways that underscore that identity. We explore ways to bring it to life and tell that story in fresh, unexpected, human and relatable ways that don't diminish the fact that we're working on things like bringing electricity to a billion people around the world".*

There is a risk here that I am teaching A-Level marketing to people who already know this stuff. But believe me, there is a huge difference between knowing and applying in the real world. To quote Benedict, 'I cannot stress strongly enough how important it is for organisations to define their brand, repeat that definition and ensure it remains congruent with that written down (publicised and referred to often) definition'.

STEP TWO. *Perceive the Audience Interest.* This next step is to identify your audience clearly. But it is much more than simply asking who they are and what impact the service you are offering will have on the business or to them in their specific roles. You need to understand the audience personally, perceive the things that will interest them and discover what will grab their attention. This is far deeper than the description I gave earlier for GE's typical audience: scientists or technologists.

We are talking about modern creative marketing here. In today's 1000-messages-per-hour world, that means it needs to emotionally snatch your audience's attention from everything else, slice through the noise and literally compel them to pay attention. You cannot do that with messages like 'this will make you more efficient in your role', or 'we offer a 30-day trial and an extended 12-month guarantee'. Doing this makes you sound just like everyone else. To cut to the heart of a B2B audience, you need to talk to the P behind the B (Person behind the Business).

Ask questions about your ideal audience like:

- What will they find interesting and/or entertaining?
- What might they look at on the tube home from work?
- Of all their social media scrolls, what might make their thumb linger the longest?

Imagine your audience as a person. One of the tricks we use is to imagine them in work clothes but on the way home. They still have one foot in the workplace, perhaps thinking about the day or what tomorrow might hold; but they are also in the process of winding down, seeing their family, going out for the evening or chilling in front of Netflix with a G&T. I believe that transitional stage is the most elucidating for a marketer in terms of understanding your audience and winning their hearts and minds.

For GE, their target market probably does have an interest in science and technology outside of work as well. But it is likely to be a more extreme, fun or expressive version of their day job. The discussion concluded that the thumb-linger moments might be things like ground-breaking innovations or really ambitious technological achievements: land-speed record attempts, the first-ever mining projects on the moon, developing the world's strongest fabric or Nikola Tesla's lost notebooks discovered at last.

STEP THREE. *Identify the Intersection.* The first two steps of the bravery in marketing model might be similar to things every marketer has encountered before. Although, I do believe there are some subtle and powerful edges to our approach. This part of the process, however, is something most marketing people miss out on entirely.

In essence, you need to identify the 'thing' that you do or the element of your company DNA that corresponds to or represents your audience's personal, visceral interest. What can you talk about that is 100% congruent with your core brand message and will capture their thumb-linger moment? Put yourself in the seat next to them on the tube, look over their shoulder and imagine what stops them in their tracks, then see if you can transpose your brand into that image. This is such an important step, and, once again, a chapter in a book cannot do it justice – it takes a team effort and unleashing your budget-free creativity.

To continue with the GE example, they concluded that their audience would be interested in stories about pushing the limits of engineering and innovation to the edge of impossible. They also decided these people probably do quite serious, high concentration jobs, carrying a weight of responsibility, so it would help if the big idea they created was fun.

STEP FOUR. *Articulate the Creative Idea.* We now have a clear target in mind and something definitive and relevant to aim for. It is not just an idea that we are looking for at this point; it is a deliberate, creative idea which the team are confident will be effective. All we need to do is find it.

This will not be the *final* big idea; it is an expression of that idea or converting the intersection discussion into a mission statement. You need to ask, what could be a mission statement that speaks to the interest through your capability and identity? Notice that I didn't say you need to create this articulation; rather, you must find it. This is an important difference because this process has turned creativity into a systematic method and presented it as a solution to a problem rather than an idea plucked out of thin air and hopeful inspiration.

GE's creative team combined their DNA (Innovation, Technology and Progress) with their target audience's interests (ground-breaking science and technology) to create an intersection (pushing the limits of engineering and innovation). I promise you; a significant amount of thought, time and questioning went into the process. But with that clarity in mind, it did not take long to arrive at an articulation of the creative idea. Making the Impossible Possible.

If you think about it in context, that is a wonderfully creative definition of innovation, *'Imagining something that is new or didn't exist previously and inventing or building it (physically or conceptually)'.* In the act of creating something new (previously impossible), you have made the impossible possible.

STEP FIVE. *Spot the Execution.* The final stage is exploring ways to creatively bring the expression to life so the right people can relate to and emotionally engage with it. There are many ways to do this, and, again, it is far too broad a subject to cover in this book, but here are a few ideas to consider. Think about something topical or ubiquitous and recognisable... or relevant to the audience. While I have said several times in this chapter to avoid copying other people's ideas, there are many cultural, topical and human references that mean something to people. It could be a familiar idiom, an anniversary or big news event, a cultural phenomenon, or reference a popular song or public figure.

Then consider how you can put *your* spin or angle on that idea to tie it to the mission statement you have created. I think it was Pablo Picasso who said, *"Good artists copy, great artists steal"*. There is nothing new under the sun, and creativity as a solution process means seeing something in one context, breaking it down, combining it with something else and applying it to a new context.

GE cracked the code by using an age-old saying that an impossible or highly unlikely outcome has a snowball's chance in hell of succeeding. After that, they applied their enormous budget to telling the story through an evocative and enthralling mini-movie to stunning effect. But that is not really the point. You (and by that, I mean any company on the planet regardless of size) could follow the process I have just described and arrive at their version of a snowball's chance in hell. Or you might arrive at asking how the person who drives the snowplough gets to work. If you are a marketer, I implore you to try this out for your business and see where you arrive.

And when you have clarity on the big idea, you don't have to hire a movie studio or travel to a foundry in Kazakhstan. You could articulate that big idea in an animation, a series of blog posts, a podcast, a green screen video, some infographics, a report, a presentation or short talk, or some interactive graphics. There are dozens of ways to get your big idea in front of the right audience. Just make sure you start by identifying what the message is.

Before I leave this chapter, I want you to consider one more thing. Most people start with the list of deliverables or executions I've listed in the previous page, based on the limitations of their budget, and say, "OK, we can afford five blog posts and a couple of infographics – what shall we talk about?" How limiting and pointless is that?

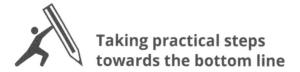

Taking practical steps towards the bottom line

Using the GE example described, apply the bravery in B2B creativity model to your own business.

Five steps to B2B creativity

1: Determine your **DNA**	2: Perceive audience **Interest**	3: Identify the **Intersection**	4: Articulate the **Creative Expression**	5: Determine your **DNA**
Why does your company exist? What's your USP?	What does your audience find interesting AND entertaining? What might they look at on the tube home from work?	How does something you do as a brand link to this interest? What expertise has a relevance?	What could be a mission statement that speaks to the interest through your capability and identity?	What's something topical or ubiquitous that your creative expression could relate to?
GE: Innovation, technology and progress...	**GE:** Ground-breaking science and technology...	**GE:** Pushing the limits of engineering and innovation	**GE:** Making the impossible possible	**GE:** "A snowball's chance in hell"
Your Brand:	**Your Brand:**	**Your Brand:**	**Your Brand:**	**Your Brand:**

CHAPTER 15

From the holiday village
to Raconteur.

If "do you want sauce with that?" serendipitously launched my sales career; it was a World War Two codebreaker's remarkable story that significantly influenced my lane-change into marketing.

After signing my escape from a rinky-dink publishing company with a Micky Mouse signature on a worthless NDA, I took up my new sales role with another publishing company. There was something about Raconteur I found compelling and irresistible from day one. It was clear there were a few problems internally (to avoid crossing unnecessary lines, I'll just say there was external pressure on the company's finances). But, the people were enthusiastic, and the work they produced was quality.

We were a young team, all early to mid-twenties, and we turned on the style. I loved selling for Raconteur in those early days and started breaking records from day one. There is no greater feeling for a salesperson than knowing you have a team behind you who will deliver the services clients need – regardless of whether those services are in the brochure before you start. Being a forward-thinking company, the directors quickly recognised my passion for innovation; and promoted me to a new (more like invented, in truth) role where I would looking at what would be next for the business. This was another of those occasions, looking back, where I can see how a level partnership with the marketing department would have accelerated what was already a very successful project.

After a couple of years, the board finally resolved the ongoing external situation that had continued to cause all manner of issues behind the scenes, and the shackles were off. It was like we had been hanging onto a lead despite a puncture but now emerged from the pit lane on a set of shiny new racing slicks.

Raconteur Publishing

Before I carry on with the story, let me give you a brief history of Raconteur Media and how the marketing agency side of the business was born.

Raconteur was founded in 2008 to publish B2B special interest reports in *The Times* and *The Sunday Times* newspapers, aimed at the eyes and ears of senior decision-makers in large organisations. This was very successful and led to around thirty reports within the first couple of years, covering future fintech, energy, and more. So, initially, the company built up a portfolio of clients buying advertising space in our reports to get in front of *The Times*' audience. We then built raconteur.net, our own publishing platform, to publish our reports digitally. Fast forward to 2022 and the publishing side of the business is absolutely thriving. We are one of the most recognisable independent B2B publishers in the world and now offer multiple products and solutions to help global B2B brands access senior business audiences.

In 2015, we were approached by several organisations like Knight Frank, Schroders and KPMG, saying, 'we love your reports in *The Times* and *Sunday Times*; can you do that for us?' If any budding young salespeople are reading this book, an important point to highlight here is: the answer to questions like that are always "Yes – give me a few days, and I'll come back to you with a proposal". So we started writing research reports, editorial reports and other custom pieces of content, building an entirely new revenue stream by seamlessly blending clients' brands with our distinct infographics, strong design and world-class content. This activity saw the birth of our Custom Publishing arm and soon developed into some branding projects, website builds and infographics and campaign-driven projects and videos. Almost by accident, this side of the Raconteur business was becoming a full-service marketing agency and found we were delivering outstanding results.

It was pretty clear we were onto a good thing pursuing the marketing agency angle. But not every new venture we launched went to plan, and sometimes those great opportunities (and even the stunningly amazing ones) need a little more thinking through before going to print. Also around 2015, we had this great idea to launch a freesheet magazine in and around London. The idea was that it would rival The Economist, with first class current affairs editorial married with eye catching graphics, but it would be free and handed out at Zone One London tube stations. We did a bit of research and gathered some feedback, and everyone (internally and externally) raved about the opportunity and potential of the plan. So, we went ahead and created a brilliant product. And I am not exaggerating, unduly blowing the Raconteur trumpet or drifting into sell-at-all-costs salesperson mode here when I say the magazine and its content was seriously good – like world-class!

But that is all that was good about it. The project itself was an unmitigated disaster, and our blind enthusiasm played a large part in the crippling losses the business suffered as a result. I am not proud of this story and am not enjoying committing it to print on these pages (remember what I said earlier about a salesperson's fragile ego), but there is a crucial point to make here, so I must complete my confession.

The magazine was ultimately a similar business model to the one we were used to through the reports we published in newspapers but had more of a current affairs flavour to the content being purely business-driven. That meant, of course, we wanted to attract a different type of advertiser through a high net worth B2C readership. Instead of selling to Microsoft and Cisco, we were looking for Cartier and Louis Vuitton, and the bottom line was that those companies were not our market. As I mentioned, we had done some research, but in hindsight, it was not the due diligence such a leap of faith deserved, regardless of how good the content was. We completely misunderstood and misjudged the commitment and timescales involved in building relationships, creating loyalty, matching buying cycles and proving a concept with high-end consumer brands. In our world, B2B clients can turn around relatively quickly, make swift decisions and get into the detail of negotiating a deal. Large B2C brands want you to get established on the agency roster, plan several seasons in advance (Christmas starts on the 1st January for most consumer brands), and don't warm particularly well to the new kid on the block.

I would like to say we quickly realised we had made a false start here, but the truth is, we sunk several months of £50-60k losses before admitting to ourselves what we knew long before the idea died. We simply didn't have the financial runway to keep going long enough and strong enough to make an impact. Six months in, we had not sold anything, and the company was looking at a black hole from which we nearly didn't return.

And yet, that magazine, in principle, was an excellent idea and a superb product. With the right due diligence, a sound commercial case (comprehensively understanding the numbers) and transparent financial backing that understood the investment cost before seeing a return, I would be telling a completely different story today. My point is that brilliant ideas, creative talent, innovative thinking and the most enthusiastic sales and marketing teams in the world are a ticking timebomb without an understanding of the numbers. I had to learn the hard way, and if I wanted to (which I don't), I could share many more examples of hard lessons my enthusiastic failings have taught me; that opportunity is only relevant in the context of profitability.

A new beginning

We rebranded from Raconteur Custom Publishing to Raconteur Agency in 2017 and continued to evolve the offering until, ironically, we bumped into a branding issue of our own. You see, the Raconteur brand is very well known as a publisher in Europe and the US, but not as an agency, and that began to confuse clients. They loved what we were doing but always asked questions and sought clarification over who, what, and why. Our key strength in both sides of the business is, of course, quality content, but the business models between a publisher and an agency are completely different. A publisher has its audience and creates its content, generating revenue through creating solutions for brands who want to engage their readership. Ultimately, Raconteur publishing is a business that is totally fixated with creating content to engage our own C-suite audiences.

On the other hand, an agency works with its clients to help them engage their audience through their owned marketing efforts. Typically, the sales process and the contract lengths for agencies are considerably longer than for publishers. So we would go through the process and present well, then when we got to the tender part of the process, clients would question why we were there. So, to progress the conversation, we had to use valuable relationship-building time and energy justifying our existence and overcoming the inevitable air of doubt. Like the carpenter whose shelves are falling down at home or the teacher whose children are struggling with their lessons, it took us longer than it perhaps should to realise we needed a rebrand.

But in August 2020, we embarked on one of the most exciting and inspiring journeys of my career to date and, from a completely blank canvas alan. agency was born. In the final chapter, I will break down the process as a *kind of* case study of a professional, innovative rebrand, and I think you'll love the story. For now, let me get back to my part in the story.

So, with this new lease of life and the business generating income that we could now invest back in accelerating that growth, the investors decided it was time for new leadership. I was effectively driving the company's agency side, and Will Brookes, my counterpart in publishing, was doing the same with the original business. Late in 2016, we were called into the boardroom and asked if we would like to buy into the company and run it properly, with more skin in the game. As I said earlier, I can't think of many scenarios where the answer to that question would be anything other than yes.

We have not looked back since, and The Raconteur Group (which includes Raconteur Media, alan. agency and Sectorlight) is now topping £12.5m in revenue per year with healthy bottom line commercials and even bigger plans for the future.

CHAPTER 16

Moving mountains: transferring marketing into the profit business.

If we are interested in learning the language of the boardroom, we must at least understand one word. It's the most important word: profit. It is not that the board is a place of mercenaries and greed; quite the opposite. The people who spend their lives guiding the ship at the forefront of the business are the custodians of everyone else's livelihood. While others lose sleep over a late report, customer complaints, or internal friction with a colleague; these heroes lie awake at night thinking about saving jobs, paying salaries, investing in the future, securing employee welfare, and ensuring there is enough in the pot to pay our pensions one day. Yes, they may earn the biggest salaries in the business, but for the most part, they earn the right because they take on the weight of responsibility. And if you want to win the board's attention, you must talk about things that give them a better night's sleep. Know your customer and market yourself to the board.

This chapter could be described as a Google Translate crash course in converting marketing-speak into the language of the board room. As a caveat, I know many people reading this book already know this stuff inside out. I am not here to teach racing drivers better-cornering; Michelin star chefs to make toast or cocktail waiters to mix drinks. But I believe the only stupid questions are those you don't ask, and I know many people fear business numbers and actively avoid contact like it's a pandemic. So, if you are supremely confident you could walk into a boardroom and comfortably engage in a conversation about the financial goals of the business and marketing's contribution to the bottom line, please feel free to skip the following 430 words. I warn you; I will be going basic.

Before you do that, here is a caveat to my caveat. If you decide to ignore this chapter because you just don't like the numbers, but you still want to be a superstar marketer who makes a difference, don't! You need to know this, and you should care.

A crash course in business numbers

Part of the problem with understanding business commercials is that different organisations and sectors use different terms to describe the same number. It is almost like they want to complicate things and create an air of black art to something that is actually quite simple. So I have tried to cover the variations here and keep the descriptions as plain English as possible.

TOTAL SALES. Also known as revenue, this is the amount of money generated through selling the company's goods and services. It does not include any other sort of income.

GROSS PROFIT. This describes the amount left after deducting the cost of making, selling and delivering a company's products or services (often referred to as COGS or cost of goods sold) from its total sales. It is sometimes called Gross Income and does not include deducting any fixed costs within the business.

OPERATING PROFIT. This describes the gross profit minus any other fixed running costs (overheads, salaries, operating expenses) associated with the business. That is all you really need to know. But for clarity, some organisations call this Operating Income or EBIT (earnings before interest and tax) because it excludes interest, tax and other non-sales related incomes or costs.) Crucially, this is also known as THE BOTTOM LINE.

Gross Profit generally includes the deduction of variable wages (including sales commissions) directly related to sales and production/ delivery volume. Operating Profit includes the deduction of any fixed salaries (not related to performance).

It would be useful to understand other terms, but a comprehensive and confident understanding of the three I have described here would be enough to hold your own. Some people struggle with this topic because the many volumes written about business numbers are by those who spent years studying the subject, gaining a plethora of university degrees. If you want to be an accountant, you can get into that stuff, but a healthy grasp of the above is an excellent place to start for a marketer and, in most cases, enough to get by. I hope that simplicity has allayed any fears for some of you, and I hope the same simplicity hasn't offended anyone who reads it as such.

I will briefly cover one more term because it can have some relevance to the marketing and sales effort.

CASH FLOW. This is important because it is possible to have a profitable business with a negative cash flow if the income (when money lands in the company bank account) arrives too long after the expenses (COGS and other costs) go out. So a sales pipeline or process (for example) where customers pay by instalments or after delivery can put the business under a degree of financial pressure.

The quality of your questions determines your stakeholder credibility

I hope the last section didn't bore you too much, and has, instead, clarified a few things in your mind. (Don't worry if it was the latter, no one else will ever know.) However, the point of that four-and-a-half-minute foundation course or recap was to set the scene for the questions you should be interested in as a revenuist marketer.

As a further caveat and clarifier, the rest of this chapter refers to organisations whose primary drive is to make a profit. Of course, there are many nuances, stages of growth, and business models in the modern world where other drivers determine the board's top level purpose and requirements. So, while each marketing department must understand those metrics and targets within their business, for clarity's sake, I am making the assumption that profit is king for now.

If marketers can accept that the numbers I've covered matter most to the people in the boardroom and want to be taken seriously as experts who contribute to the bottom line, they must change the board's minds. I speak from experience when I say that most boardrooms see marketing as a nice-to-have whose primary function is to make their assets look good. If you are still reading this book, I can only hope it is because you know that shouldn't be the case, and you want to make sure everyone else knows how critical marketing is to the bottom line. You need to show everyone outside of the marketing department how much you understand why marketing exists.

In chapters thirteen and fourteen, I talked about escaping the bounds of the budget and thinking creativity-first. But I also suggested marketers should measure their own contribution internally and create ways to prove their value externally. This could come in the shape of self-regulation (measuring the marketing metrics that matter to the department) while also demonstrating your understanding of the critical business metrics by only showing the board the numbers that matter to them. In other words, self-questioning before asking others' opinions or waiting for negative feedback. For example, logic and vanity dictate that generating 1000 leads is better than 400 leads. No one could dispute it is a more significant number to show the board. But what if the marketing team had examined this contribution against the bottom line opportunity? What if the 400 leads represented the genuine SQL (Sales Qualified Leads: the sales team's exact criteria) proportion of the total and the other 600 were just names on a spreadsheet. Yes, the lower number is not as impressive; but it represents the real value and sharing it honestly with the board will demonstrate the department's clarity on delivering where it counts.

It is a well-known, often neglected fact that it costs less time, effort and financial expense to market to existing customers than find new ones. Equally acknowledged is that the emotional barriers to reaching these customers are significantly lower because they have already exchanged money for products and services at least once – especially the happy ones. Yet, despite this accepted wisdom, most B2B marketers spend the majority of their efforts winning new business because that is the sexier headline. It may not be the case in all organisations, but it is worth investigating the return on investment (bottom-line profitability) opportunities gained from marketing to existing customers. Spending more time in this area might even increase the lifetime value of that customer by prolonging the length of the relationship: repeat business is good, but cross-selling and upselling is even better. And it might only take an email (unremarkable and hardly cutting edge digital marketing) to generate that highly profitable sale. I realise this doesn't sound like a result worth breaking out the fireworks, but I promise you, presenting metrics like this to a boardroom (supported by a bottom-line contribution business case) will turn heads and open ears. And, as I have covered earlier in the book, once you have their grown-up attention, you can start the creativity-first conversation.

Things like this demonstrate that a marketer is thinking about business commercially and the end-to-end value they contribute to its targets. It shows they are not just the colouring-in department gathering likes and leads to hand over to the sales team and then wash their hands of the matter.

Working backwards along the Awareness-To-Profit funnel

Every pound of revenue sitting in an organisation's bottom line profit account started life in a customer's pocket long before they knew the company existed. If we are splitting hairs, it began in the Royal Mint or when some Chancellor of the Exchequer borrowed or invented it, but you know what I mean. Most people in that organisation never take the time to consider the journey from awareness to profit – but those who care about the business should. I believe everyone in every company should receive a version of the education I am about to share with you because it should influence how they do their job.

It doesn't matter what role you play in your business; you will generate a positive or adverse effect on its bottom-line profitability. And that, in turn, will affect the security of your role, your chances of promotion or pay rise, the working standards and safety within the business, the quality of people employed to work alongside you and the opportunities, perks and freedom on offer. The fact is, all these things are determined by how profitable an organisation is: because the cash available to spend on growth, investment, environment and developing the business comes from that pot.

From the accounts department to the cleaners, HR to logistics, the facilities team to marketing, all impact how much cash is retained each year. Something as small as the cleaners putting the bins back in the right places after emptying them can save a busy HR Manager with OCD tendencies 10-minutes per day (1-hour per week, or a week per year) of fixing their environment before they can start work. These things add up and make a difference.

The solution is to look beyond what matters to you in your immediate role and see how your actions impact the world around you. For marketers, the day-to-day activities that matter most tend to be:

BRAND AWARENESS. A key activity for the marketing team is brand activation. Ensuring the right people see the company's name in the right places, read good news, watch the adverts, notice the straplines, remember the message and slowly learn to trust the ubiquitous certainty of the brand.

PROSPECT ENGAGEMENT. The marketing team then transforms that awareness into interactions, reactions, and recognition, moving the relationship from know to like, and skillfully through to trust.

COLLECTING LEADS. For many marketers, this is the end goal. It's where their part in the complexity of the greater business vision ceases to have any meaning. (Another caveat: I know this is not the case for all, but it is more common than most will admit.) The handover of leads to sales is often the job-done-move-on moment.

I understand why most people working in a marketing role today take this viewpoint. The headline or end goal in their job description, below the job title and the day-to-day activities, dictates it. But marketing is far more important than vanity metrics set by people who don't understand the business-critical value of the profession either. That pigeon-holed limitation is killing marketing, internally and externally, and education is needed to reposition the situation.

Good marketers intuitively take their responsibility one step further along the Awareness-To-Profit funnel. They cultivate the next step:

CONVERSATIONS. This is when a marketer delivers a salesperson's dream and qualifies the leads before passing them on. By having conversations (verbal, digital or both), the marketing team identifies if the lead is the right person or organisation (needs the solution and has the means or authority to make the purchase) for the sales team to set up a meeting.

Organisations with marketing teams who move leads into conversations or SQLs before carefully handing them over to the sales team are very fortunate indeed. That extra step massively benefits the company, but what about the marketer? What do they get out of that relationship? Let me explain the rest of the journey towards creating profit, and then I'll come back to how marketers can and should be rewarded for their endeavours.

A2P: Awareness-To-Profit funnel

We have covered the first four steps, and now we reach the four that most marketers do not consider relevant to their roles. Let's look at them briefly now:

PIPELINE. Traditionally, this is the domain of the sales team, and it would take a brave and swashbuckling marketer to venture into that territory unarmed. It is the place where salespeople duck and dive, spin and sell, fact-find and follow-up, present and persuade as they attempt to take leads on a journey to the dotted line.

SALES. Whenever you hear that cheer go up from inside the sales department door, it indicates a sale has closed, or a deal is done. As I described in the Salesperson's Psyche chapter, there is nothing quite like that feeling of relief and success when it all comes together in a sale. Salespeople live for these moments.

I have discussed utilising CRM systems in previous chapters, describing how marketers can follow leads through the sales pipeline (or funnel) and support, advise or add value to the sales effort to reach a sale. These powerful tools can also help to learn from and finetune any marketing activity and collateral for the future. Creativity and connection with clients and prospects also mean being agile and fast to adapt to the needs and motivations of the marketplace.

GROSS PROFIT AND OPERATING PROFIT. As described earlier, these numbers are the language spoken in the boardroom and are the defining moments in every single employee's career.

This chapter will, I hope, have shown you how all of the activities mentioned matter to the marketing department. And the best way to use the information is to reverse engineer your marketing activities based on the end-goal objectives of the business as a whole – profit. That is how you move the needle and become famous.

This sort of thinking will reinforce the importance and reliance on marketing at the highest levels. And the more you make yourself irreplaceable and show your contribution to the bottom line, the more powerful your hand becomes when negotiating a fair share of the bonus structure.

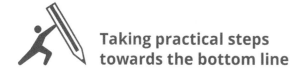

Taking practical steps towards the bottom line

Here are some questions you could ask to help clarify marketing's influence on the two profit numbers in the Awareness-To-Profit funnel. Answer these questions for your business and see if you can think of any more. This information could also be used to strengthen your conversations with various departments and influencers throughout the business (as described in the practical section of chapter eight - Knowing the customer behind the data). Imagine the impact of sharing these metrics with the people who set the budget in your organisation.

- How does the marketing department's spend translate into cost per acquisition?
- What factors determined the last budget we received, and how can I challenge the number?
- What does revenue per headcount mean for our business, and why does it matter?
- Do we really understand the SQL definition in our business, and could a conversation with sales help?
- How could we help sales to make closing deals more profitable or increase positive cash flow?
- What would a marketing-bonus structure look like in our business, and why would it work?
- What are the metrics that will grab the board's attention and make marketing impossible to ignore?

CHAPTER 17

Claim your stake as a
marketer of the future.

In this book, I have introduced the idea of a new type of marketer — the revenuist. I don't particularly care whether that title catches on in the wider world and becomes a 'thing' on LinkedIn. But what I do care about is the marketers' position within their organisations. That *must* change – without question! Armed with your newfound (or recapped) knowledge of business numbers and the language of the boardroom from the last chapter, I now want to explore how to make marketing famous. In truth, the whole book has been building up to this chapter. This is the one where I want marketers to self-examine and commit to moving the needle in their world.

So, we will now focus on what a good marketer actually looks like in the modern commercial world. In doing this, I hope to describe what today's ambitious young marketers need to focus on to equip themselves for a successful future as true, rounded and grounded marketers, not back-office administrators.

We have talked about the need for marketers to be more aligned with salespeople in their organisation. That means opening and strengthening communication channels, showing a little empathy for the salespeople and their side of the coin and even mirroring a few (not too many) of their more robust characteristics. And we discussed how taking the initiative, or the first step, in this relationship will compel good salespeople to recognise the commercial benefit to them and respond in kind.

I introduced the idea of the BCB Pill, where marketers educate themselves daily on the commercial BUSINESS; exercise some big picture CREATIVITY over mere activity, and apply a little BACKBONE by doing something bold and ambitious whenever possible.

We then looked at the customer relationship and how to take it beyond the data and closer to the people who actually make the decisions. No one can question the data (numbers do not lie after all), and forecasting trends will always be more accurate alongside analysis of the past and current. But the reality is that we must translate technical data into emotional intelligence to grasp the bigger picture of our customers' needs. We also entered the boardroom arena to discuss the things that matter to the people who make the decisions and decide both marketing's future and how marketing is allowed to do its work and prove its worth. I even turned to my colleague, Benedict Buckland, to share some of his expertise on bravery in B2B marketing.

Underpinning all of these views, insights, and the essential toolkit I have presented was the Marketer's Hierarchy of Needs model, which I introduced in chapter two. Would you indulge me and return to that now? Because I would like to think this book will guide your way up to the Creativity and Influence levels of that model, at the very least. (I'm not promising you will get there by the time you reach the final page, but I do believe it will help you create a roadmap for the future and a one, two or three-year plan you can start working out today.)

The Marketer's Hierarchy of Needs

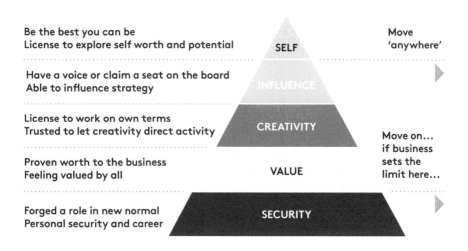

So, with some practical guides, ideas and strategies under our belt, let's look at the seven personality traits of a great marketer or marketing revenuist. If you are ambitious to become better, recognise that change is necessary for the marketing profession, and *want* to create an environment in your business where you can be a creative marketer, spend a little time each day developing these attributes for yourself:

1. INQUISITIVE. In our rapidly changing, high-speed world, no other principle will serve you better (in a marketing career or any area of life) than acknowledging you don't know what you don't know. That means you are constantly on the lookout for ways that will lead you to unknown information, simply because you realise no one will offer up what is to them an obvious or already accepted fact. These discoveries are often called black swans, a metaphor to describe things that no one even considered a possibility before they existed. For centuries swans were only ever considered to be white birds. Various species of swan were known throughout ornithology, but every single variation was always white, and no one had any reason to imagine an alternative. (Perhaps a brave and creative marketing team, escaping the bounds of its budget somewhere in the seventeenth century, might have come up with the idea one day. But they too would have surely discarded such an obscure absurdity.) Then one day in the summer of 1697, the Dutch explorer Willem de Vlamingh landed on a beach in Western Australia, and before him, he witnessed the impossible in all its beautiful glory. Black swans, the unimaginable variation of a common occurrence, became a reality. He had discovered what no one (other than the people who lived there and thought all swans were black) knew that they didn't know. In the same way, a great marketer should be an explorer of undiscovered truths. Someone who uncovers solutions in one part of the world they can apply within their own. Be inquisitive every day, ask good questions, and you will discover more than you thought possible.

2. HOLISTIC. To be the best marketer you can be, you have to stop looking through a marketer's lens. Totally counter-intuitive and within the context of this book, pretty ironic, I know. Every company consists of multiple departments, influences, drivers and personalities. The whole point of this book is to position marketing at the very heart of a business and as the most critical of those facets – because that is where I believe it should exist. And to do that, the people who run and work in marketing departments must understand: their position is a responsibility to the business. Your company needs you. No other department has access to the same level of internal and external data and relationships to understand what is required to drive the business forward. So marketing professionals must look through a holistic lens to equip themselves for the role they are designed to fulfil.

3. SALES AWARE. As I covered in detail in the first half of this book, marketing and sales are two sides of the same coin, and I cannot stress how important it is for the two departments to work closely together. It should be a two-way effort, but the nature of salespeople means marketers will usually need to make the first move to build the relationship, and only a stubborn marketer will let their pride get in the way of letting that happen. After all, marketing departments will benefit just as much as sales in the long run. Developing greater awareness of salespeople and the sales process makes for a powerful attribute in a marketing person. Remember how we discussed being more purple and why it is crucial for marketing to make an effort to bridge the divide and learn more about sales? (Unfortunately it simply will not work the other way around.)

4. COURAGEOUS. The thing about creativity is that you have to put new ideas out there. And that means dedicating time to formulate new ideas. No matter how under pressure you are or the other demands on your time, the role of marketing is to be creative. And you cannot do that unless you allocate serious time for thinking about the audience you are trying to reach and the problem you are trying to solve for them. Anything new comes with an element of risk. Others might not understand your vision or how you have approached a project, and be prepared to accept that some will not be as open to new thinking as you. So, to be brave and adventurous as a marketer, you need to have confidence in yourself and your ability. Speaking as a former salesperson whose livelihood depended on taking risks and winning most of the time, I have learned that failure or missing the target is an inevitable part of the winning process. As soon as you accept that you will not always win, it becomes easier to manage failure courageously. Don't get me wrong, I hate losing – but I know that each loss is only taking me closer to a win. That simple piece of knowledge is all I need to be confident, adventurous and willing to put my ideas out there.

5. HONEST. There really is no point in trying to convince others you are something or someone you don't believe in yourself. Self-belief is a compelling asset in business. It can turn comedians into rappers, YouTubers into boxers and even second-rate businessmen into presidents. Do not underestimate where a combination of honesty and believing in yourself can take you. The truth will always come out eventually, and pretending you care when you don't is hard work and ultimately unsustainable. For me, honesty goes hand in hand with courage and being adventurous because believing in an end goal means you will keep fighting until you get there. So, if the ideals and potential I have presented in this book appeal to you, I would ask you to have a good look in the mirror and question if you are up for the fight. I promise you everything I have suggested is possible because, as a salesperson who runs a successful City marketing agency, I have seen first-hand what great marketers are capable of achieving. But, at no point have I suggested the journey is easy. It takes hard work, courage and honesty to become the best.

6. COMMERCIALLY SAVVY. This list is essentially about character traits rather than skills and abilities. But I have included understanding commercials and business numbers because I believe it is a state of mind that turns some people away from mastering this critical knowledge. The more you tell yourself you don't like the commercial aspect of business, the more you will believe it to be true. I hope the simple explanations I offered in the previous chapter have taken the edge off the fear and opened the door for more marketers to be open to them. And I am also convinced that when marketers start to see the genuine impact they have on those numbers growing, they will begin to embrace them and look forward to shouting about how their efforts can positively influence the bottom line.

7. ACCOUNTABILITY. This is a big one for me because I believe we increasingly live in a blame culture where the first instinct is to look outside to find fault when something goes wrong. One of the big things being a salesperson has taught me is that I can always do better. I have been guilty of blaming the quality of leads or the lack of people to speak to, and I could write an entire book about the array of salespeople's excuses I have used or heard from others. But even when there are outside influences, I could still do more myself. It is always possible to make the most of a bad situation, just as it is equally possible to capitalise on good fortune. If everyone in an organisation were to become fully accountable for their own efforts, they and everyone around them would benefit. And in the same way that I believe marketing should be leading a company's business strategy, I think a sign of a great marketer is to hold themselves accountable for their work. As an example, I would refer you back to the Marketer's Hierarchy of Needs model. If you follow the steps I've laid out in this book courageously, honestly and holistically, and the business still doesn't recognise your value, go and find an employer who will.

Taking practical steps towards the bottom line

Now repeat the same exercise from chapter two and reassess both your current position and the steps you need to take to progress to the levels where your ambition wants to be.

Use the questions and criteria in this practical section to identify your current position on the Marketer's Hierarchy of Needs model. Then decide where you would like to go and your career and start to think about the steps you can take to get there.

Your hierarchy of needs as a marketer

1. .... SELF
2. ....

1. .... INFLUENCE
2. ....

1. .... CREATIVITY
2. ....

1. .... VALUE
2. ....

1. .... SECURITY
2. ....

1. Where do you think you are now?

2. What needs to happen to move up a level?

Notes:

Do you have SECURITY in your role? Do you believe you have clarity about these things within your role?

- Do you have a defined role and clear responsibilities? Do you know what is expected of you?
- Key Performance Indicators - allowing you and your managers to measure if you deliver a result.

Success at this level should begin to create a sense of security that your role is secure.

Write a few lines to describe what needs to happen for you to fulfil this criteria and move to the next level:

....

....

....

....

....

....

....

....

....

....

....

Are you VALUED within the team? Can you recognise and demonstrate the value you bring to your role?

- Do you see how you fit within the broader marketing team? Whose work does your work influence?
- Learn where your output benefits the results and identify the part you play in the bigger picture.
- Decide if others recognise your contribution. How can you make sure your efforts are seen?

In a perfect world, we would all like to think others see us for the value we bring. But we do not live in a perfect world, so take a leaf from the salesperson's playbook and find ways to make your results shine.

Write a few lines to describe what needs to happen for you to fulfil this criteria and move to the next level:

....

....

....

....

....

....

....

....

....

Can you work CREATIVELY off-piste? Is your voice heard and respected within the team?

- Are all your tasks tick-box exercises or are you afforded the freedom to experiment?
- Can you begin to define your own role, where the result is more important than the means?
- Do your peers ask your opinion and are you part of the broader marketing conversation?

When you are asked your opinion and get involved in the broader conversation around the direction of the marketing team's efforts, you can call yourself a true marketer.

Write a few lines to describe what needs to happen for you to fulfil this criteria and move to the next level:

Does your INFLUENCE reach beyond marketing? Does your work and your voice get noticed beyond marketing?

- Can you converse with your sales team with commercial parity or do you feel they look down on you? ☐
- Can you converse with the board or other heads of departments with commercial parity? ☐
- Can you describe your department's contribution to the business with 100% confidence and pride? ☐

This book is about putting marketers in a place where they can drive the business forward from the inside. To do that you need to be in the driving seat and that means stepping outside of the marketing department and having bigger conversations with other business leaders.

Write a few lines to describe what needs to happen for you to fulfil this criteria and move to the next level:

....

....

....

....

....

....

....

....

....

Where do you want to go as a marketer? Are you happy and fulfilled in what you are doing?

- Could you do more with your position? Could you use your influence to push the business further forward?
- Where else could you take the business or your career as a marketer or entrepreneur?

My ambition is for this model, and the rest of the content in this book, to encourage and guide marketers to the strategic forefront of their organisations and drive their careers and opportunities to new heights.

Write a few lines to describe what needs to happen for you to fulfil this criteria and move to the next level:

....

....

....

....

....

....

....

....

....

....

....

CHAPTER 18

Ok Rich, Where do I start?

My sincere hope is that the pages of this book have resonated with you on some level and prompted you to want to take action. Maybe you lead a marketing team and want to share these thoughts with them so they can support your drive for a place on the board. Or you could be a graduate in your first year of a role in a marketing department: deciding if you are up for the challenge of becoming famous and claiming your voice. Whatever your view, or your current position, I don't believe anyone in marketing can afford to bury their head in the sand and hope it all turns out OK.

And I also know I am not alone in those beliefs. So, in this chapter, I have invited some of the people I speak to regularly, whose opinions and achievements I trust and admire, to contribute some of their thoughts and experiences.

WINNIE PALMER

Winnie is currently Head of Marketing at Seismic. She has led and transformed GTM functions across a number of the industry's most prominent technology brands, including HPE, Huawei, Microsoft and Nokia, driving digital transformation and scaling business growth. She is also a board member at the University of Greenwich and an advisor for start-up firms.

I've always looked at marketers as the builders of an organisation as, beyond content and campaigns, most marketers also have operations, processes, infrastructure and the tech stack in our scope. So it's only natural for us to find solutions that help ensure integration across sales and marketing becomes a business reality.

In my experience at Seismic, my team sits between product, customers and sales, bringing Seismic's pioneering sales enablement solutions to market in a way that adds real value to all stakeholders, including customers and prospective buyers. It is precisely this "outside-in" and "inside-out" view that gives marketing a voice in the commercial engine. This helps ensure each component within the go-to-market motion is well-aligned.

That concept of value applies throughout our work. Ultimately, alignment between sales and marketing needs to happen at the interpersonal level beyond processes and data. Trust is critical. Therefore, I believe it's useful for marketing to demonstrate value and continuously make it visible to sales teams. For example, the collaboration between B2B sales and marketing can be anchored around new pipeline generation – sales cannot live without pipeline, and marketing is the powerhouse that drives pipelines at scale.

Experience also tells me there's something to be said about intelligence and analytics. By injecting market-led insights directly into the business's go-to-market thought process, marketers will be able to influence and shape commercial strategy internally and drive demand and adoption at scale externally. This level of retail leadership is invaluable to businesses operating in today's fast-moving world with ever-changing market dynamics and competitive landscapes. Having the agility to move between strategy, tactics and across functions is something any marketer worth their salt would likely say are critical skills to succeed. Context matters, and marketers understand this.

The most effective working relationships I have built have always been underpinned by considered insights that add to a conversation. For example, in B2B SaaS, it is fashionable to talk about paths to growth, and there are frameworks about how best to do that. But every business is different. One size does not fit all!

For example, one of the B2B SaaS businesses I worked for did very well with an inbound-first approach as its products were suitable for this GTM model, whereas another firm focused on enterprise sales first. Savvy marketers can analyse different business contexts to create differentiated commercial models and GTM approaches that meet specific business needs.

One last thing I want to comment on is creativity. Many methodologies are available to help model what marketing spending would be appropriate. That aside, I am a true believer that budget is not a prerequisite for creativity. Ingenuity and creative thinking are what marketers can always lean into to bring real impact to the market – creating a long-term view of the business over what's needed. Socialising that to generate momentum while being super practical with execution can deliver value and achieve a marketer's mission.

PAUL COLLIER

Paul is a Marketing leader with 25 years+ of experience working for large tech brands, including Dell, HPE and IFS.

My advice to marketers is first to understand the business, the characteristics of the P&L, and its variability according to geography, product, industry segment, or even customer size compared to whatever is the "norm" in your company, including the people, partners, suppliers, agencies etc.

The P&L, in its various guises, becomes the eyes of a business. So if you can look at it and pick up the nuances, you will have a realistic shot of developing a demonstrable effect.

Secondly, review the capabilities you have in place; the personnel, the agencies, ecosystem, and partners locally, regionally, and globally (or centrally). Ideally, they must be supported or underpinned by the necessary technology and tools. You should never limit their capabilities because the CRM is poor or the marketing automation is not up to spec.

To share an example of this working: when the GM of the company I had just joined (part of a Fortune 50 global IT company) said, "The marketing function globally and locally has little credibility in my business leadership and the wider sales team. We've hired you for one main reason... fix it" I saw that as a challenge that could be overcome.

The business segment in question had always been considered a corporate outlier. Known as mavericks, they didn't conform to the broader corporate constraints based on costs such as travel, meetings etc. Its P&L was growing at 2x the business average in revenue terms and all whilst delivering 3 to 4 times the margins, becoming the cash cow of the organisation. Each sales organisation had a differing profile of needs based on their varying contribution to the P&L, and each team had a differing profile of engagement.

I could see there were issues on both sides. However, in some cases, marketing had missed the nuances in what was delivered and had delivered broad brush activities.

What followed over subsequent quarters was my first commercialisation of marketing. I ensured sales and marketing understood they were 'in it together.' Ultimately, we were all being paid on the top line P&L metrics and sat equal partners when the issues and opportunities arose. (Those issues and opportunities will always vary according to the specific commercial pattern of that part of the business.)

The outcome? We developed the first "ABM" approach (bear in mind this was c2010) as a regional marketing function, leading to a globally adopted system in this area. A year later, I was asked to stand in as a regional leader, a first for the marketing function in that or another business.

IRIS MEIJER

When she was global CMO of Verizon Business, Iris Meijer spearheaded the launch of the Vodafone Business brand and built the first-ever pan-European SME strategy.

I've always been passionate about marketing and its essential role in a company's success. However, I've found myself in too many peer discussions centred around the challenges marketers face in getting their voices heard: some have even suggested we should not attempt to find a link between marketing activities and company revenues because it's just too difficult. Surrounded by these clever, incredibly talented go-getters, I wondered what was going on and what I could do to change this mindset and promote the relevance and importance of marketing.

As marketers, we seem to rate ourselves lower than our peers on the board rate us. In fact, as low as 5% of marketers are confident they can influence the direction of the business they work for. When you compare this to the 55% of CEOs who believe they can, that's quite a shocking difference!

But as many marketing organisations have demonstrated through the global pandemic, we have earned our spot at the top table. We are empowered to make strategic and commercially informed decisions by going deeper into the customer data.

We're mastering the balance between science and art that goes hand in hand with our profession. With data, we can explain the more creative and purpose-driven choices that we're making and prove our effectiveness to our colleagues on the board.

The global pandemic changed the course of economies, communities, and consumer and business behaviours. Companies revisited their roles and responsibilities in societies and how to communicate with their customers. These challenges have brought opportunities for CMOs to make a real difference in the boardroom.

Effective marketing requires us to be closer than ever to our customers and the societies we serve. Our peers on the board have looked to marketers to draw upon our customer knowledge and get our commercial response right in a time of crisis.

These drivers accelerated marketing to take on a more strategic role, with a massive shift in the importance of customer insight almost overnight. Having a view of customer data and analysing that data has guided my role in making more informed decisions and constantly evolving our approach.

In many organisations, marketing led the approach during the peak of the crisis, guiding what to say, how to say it and developing propositions based on customer knowledge. As a result, we now have a significant role in shaping the company's strategic direction. There has been a realisation that marketers are the guardians of the customer – we have the knowledge and a deep understanding of their needs.

Marketers should have confidence in their existing strengths and develop commercial acumen to break out of being seen as a support function. Commercial acumen is vital for modern marketing, and we have more data than ever before to back up our choices.

The link between the art and the science in marketing has never been more in focus than now. Great business and commercial strategies are powered by customer insight and delivered by creative tactics. Unfortunately, no one else on the board can take this on – so it's time to believe in ourselves and live up to the promise that a modern marketer can deliver.

TOM ANDREWS

Tom is a recognised expert in technology and revenue operations with experience architecting funnels for multiple successful xtech/SaaS scale-ups.

With over 8000 technologies in the marketing technology landscape, more platforms and channels than ever before and more data than anyone knows what to do with, the place to start is not trying to get your head around all of that. You'll fail.

The best place to start is, as always, at the finish line. Start where you mean to end up - at the bottom line. Then it's a matter of working backwards through your funnel to work out what you need to put in to get that out. Simple, no?

No. As a revenue technologist who has been successfully knitting together sales and marketing teams and technologies for years, I know all too well that this isn't as easy as it sounds. Funnels are ever more complex beasts that amalgamate more tools every day and transform data in ways few will ever truly grasp. In that respect, marketing and sales technology is the final frontier of enterprise tech. We're predicting the outcome of an unknown number of actions across a journey of unspecified length and navigating an unknown number of information points. Strangely, however, we're succeeding. As daunting as it sounds, as many assumptions as you may need to plug in and as much of your sanity as you may lose - embracing technology and putting it to work is the most important thing you can do.

And the data agrees with me. This year, in the 2021 Gartner CMO Spend Survey, we saw Martech accounting for 26.6% of the total marketing expense budget allocation. Further, when drilling down into marketing programs and operational areas, marketing operations and marketing analytics ranked second and fourth, respectively, with 22.9% of the allocation.

Technology isn't the answer, but it has all the answers you seek. To work with sales, you need to build a seamless, end-to-end funnel encompassing the whole revenue process. Gone are the days of showing a simple primary lead source. How can you tell the story of a prospect and how they came to be interested in your product or service? What were the inflection points, points of interest and how have they resulted in interest? How can this vital context form part of the story that your sales team can tell? When you've answered all these questions, it's time for the next level—multi-touch marketing attribution. It's the holy grail of marketing operations but a worthy undertaking. There are more ways of implementing this with modern technology than ever before - but that's the most significant part of the challenge. How can you, as a marketer, become the expert in your own data? As you scale your operations, how can you follow the golden brick road through your systems, weaving the threads together to tell the story of your customer? Then show, empirically and objectively, where your campaigns, tactics and programs impacted that tapestry at every step of the way?

As for working with sales, it's a simple matter of remembering that, together, you're co-authoring the stories of your customers. Between these two departments that will undoubtedly end up as one, you are the custodians of the customer journey. In an increasingly complex market, customers need to be guided through the morass of information by trusted advisors. Once there were clear lines between sales and marketing, but demand generation, account-based programs, and revenue analytics have blurred, if not erased, them altogether. Going forwards, customers need to be at the heart of the revenue engine. It's up to both sales and marketing, who often know the customers best, to advocate for them and work together to make their journeys the best they can be.

Together, you need to find your way through the successful sales and marketing technology markets to build a funnel you can operationalise that brings harmony and helps to reveal the full stories of your customers. However, should you get lost on the way to the funnel of your dreams, fear not. We're out here - the king-makers of revenue functions across the globe. Whether you want to call us sales, revenue or marketing operations, we're one of the fastest-growing professions on the planet. And building funnels? That's what we do.

JULIE FEWELL

Julie is a senior marketing professional with over 20 years of experience working for start-ups, growing businesses, and complex global organisations for several organisations. She has a wealth of experience developing go-to-market strategies, helping companies build relationships with their clients, drive revenues, and create innovative campaigns and programmes.

Much of my experience has been in professional services, where it's not uncommon for marketers to hear, "I need to build my profile", "I want to write a blog", or "we need to run a webinar" or "here's a 50-page report we've developed, can you take this to market". Whilst we want to be seen as strategic and adding value, there is still some confusion about marketing and its role within a business.

Who is at fault here? Is it the marketer for not positioning themselves clearly in the mind of the business and their stakeholders? Or is it the rest of the business who see the marketing department as the people who are there to 'do things'? Or a bit of both, perhaps?

Unfortunately, if you're not close enough to the business, involved in the right discussions and able to show how marketing adds value to the business, pipeline, Net Promote Score (NPS), and overall bottom line etc., there is a chance that you'll continue to be asked to do these types of things.

The good news is that, as marketers, we're well-positioned to change this.

Modern marketers are data-driven. One of my favourite quotes is "Without data, you're just another person with an opinion" [from Dr W. Edwards Deming]. We have access to lots of data and feel comfortable getting into the detail and using it to help form conversations with stakeholders.

There is nothing better than attending a meeting armed with data and insight to back up what you're going to say. You're no longer 'just another person with an opinion'.

Marketers also tend to be naturally curious. We like to ask questions and build relationships with people both inside the business and with clients. We can help bring valuable insight and see potential connections with the data that others might not have.

I think it's a great time to be a marketer, but we need to be braver. Braver in pushing back on activities we know add little value and braver in pushing ourselves forward more, using data and insight to make informed decisions.

PHILIPPE RUTTENS

B2B marketing consultant and interim manager Philippe Ruttens transforms B2B sales and marketing teams into revenue marketing centres of excellence. For the last 25 years, he has been helping international scale-ups, and mid-size enterprises grow their brand, leads and revenue in 10+ sectors across Belgium, Netherlands, Germany, UK and US.

Digital marketing and transformation have now been top-of-mind for these last 20 years. However, B2B marketing teams are still lagging way behind their B2C counterparts in many ways.

Over the last 15 years and still, in 2021, I have witnessed that most B2B Marketing teams are suffering from five key gaps:

1. Limited integration and teamwork with their Sales and Business Development counterparts
2. Poor measurement and focus on sales and buyer KPIs (vs only top-funnel ones)
3. Lack of proper revenue marketing and demand generation skills, with too many marketers staying stuck in their "Marcom, design and branding" comfort zone
4. Content marketing remains underleveraged in terms of relevance, personalisation, lead experience, production agility and impact on the buyer journey
5. Insufficient customer insights, marketing data and tech-based decision-making

To solve these issues, it's vital that the CMO or VP of marketing connects all the dots, from customer experience to sales enablement and account-centricity, under a data-based, responsive revenue growth vision and operations. Equally important is how aligned our marketing leads are with their CEO, CFO, CIO and CCO.

Without those crucial elements, the whole marketing team will never reach their full potential and, even worse, will crash and burn in 2022 due to a lack of measurable impact on their company's bottom line.

B2B marketing "teams of the future" need to think ecosystem and hybrid, which means three core principles:

1. Expand their scope and vision to integrate clients, prospects, contractors, influencers, communities, partners and even competitors in their go-to-market plan
2. Build a fluid, on-demand team of core talent mixing freelance/interim senior experts, specialised boutique agencies and own core talent for execution
3. Plan, implement and optimise in monthly and quarterly timeframes instead of yearly ones. Think dashboards, sprints, campaigns and content execution as core weapons.

I would summarise five trends more as key levers and enablers for transforming from a 2010s marketing to a 2022s Revenue Ops team:

1. Refocus from pure Lead Gen and "growth hacking" to more integrated "smart inbound", content-based buyer experiences
2. Measure and optimise marketing impact on account and sales opportunities creation vs traditional KPIs
3. Less automated pure-digital outreach and more manual, human-based storytelling approach
4. Increased focus on leveraging true client and prospect intent signals through better first-party (own) data instead of generic and limited second and third-party data
5. Evolution of ABM 2.0 into engagement and opportunity-based marketing due to sales focus

B2B marketing teams need to generate or analyse better, faster insights and data about audiences. This can be done by mixing human, manual research with AI and all first, second and third-party tools available, such as website add-ons like LeadFeeder, HotJar, and HubSpot.

A key priority is developing a structured, weekly framework for gathering buyer insights and journey behaviour to inform campaigns and content strategy. This will then feed a personalisation approach adapted to clusters (1-Few) vs (1-1) due to more expansive buying centres and deeper, complex journeys.

To enable this, a "fit for purpose" MarTech stack needs to integrate with SalesTech into a true RevOps set of tools and processes used daily by all teams. This will energise a tighter (people) integration with Sales, CSM, Account Management around data and insights and help you refocus your content and campaigns accordingly.

Finally, investing in better, more personalised tactics: such as social and chatbots using human and emotional (vs automated) messages based on triggers and events, will allow B2B marketers to keep their finger on the buyer and client journey at best. Examples include progressive profiling of challenges, pain points and educational needs through short, question-based emails. In addition, interactive and visual ways to engage prospects personally (incl. career-boosting tools) are also in demand.

Calculators, guides, blog posts, eBooks, case studies etc., are still needed. But from 2022, think "dark social" first such as those hard-to-reach, tough-to-measure private communities and channels where experts and their peers share stories and questions about your brand. Helping customers by answering practical questions or providing tips without selling your products shows your personality and human approach. It's how brands are built, talked about, and trusted by your target audience, not through "push" LinkedIn InMails, banner ads, or lead gen forms.

This means showing your content at the right place and time and with the correct consumption format and emotional angle to win the brand trust and conversion to deals.

CHAPTER 19

2020 is not an option!

Most of our lives changed during the COVID-19 pandemic that hit us like a bullet train in 2020 and has continued casting its influence worldwide ever since. But, while much of the world feared over life, livelihood and what happens next, and businesses large and small closed their doors or folded in on themselves, some organisations thrived.

Throughout history, it has always been the case that every disaster or hardship for the majority will create opportunity and profit for a minority. I'm not glorifying this, necessarily, just stating it as a reality. And regardless of the impact lockdown, restrictions and circumstances had on your life personally or the lives of those you love, the history books will record 2020 and 2021 as a year the world would rather forget. But here is what we do need to remember: change, challenges, and catastrophes have been responsible for every significant shift in direction throughout the history of humanity. As a collective race, we prefer consistency and do not embrace change unless we have no other choice. Who would have imagined as we approached Christmas 2019 that the following one would have been (in effect) cancelled? No one would have believed as we came to March 2020 that 'working from home' would cease to be a 'thing' because almost everyone who was working was doing so from home – it became routine. And the very idea that our revered cathedrals of sport could be silenced, as adoring fans sang and walked alone from the comfort of their living room floor, seemed ludicrous in the extreme. We wouldn't have believed these things possible, but they happened, we adapted, and most people soon settled into the rhythm of the new normal. It was not by choice, but even as I write this chapter, I can see evidence of cost efficiencies, environmental benefits and improvements in working practices within our business.

Marketing needs to change! The way things were in 1980, 1990, 2000, 2010 and 2020 cannot continue. Like everyone else, marketing professionals could easily work from their home office, garden shed or pyjamas and bedside cabinet during 2020 and 2021, but that is not the change I am talking about. And I fear the essential wake-up call needed will not come until it is too late and half the profession has fallen asleep or drifted into administration. That is why I wrote this book. I know many top marketing professionals have noticed the warning signs, too, even though some of them thrived during the pandemic. But I believe average marketers haven't seen what is coming. In fact, I think the biggest shakeup marketing has ever seen is already here. The savvy marketers are out there now... stealing the show and making headlines: while the majority, those average marketers, are still patting themselves on the back for page views. I predict the latter will not even exist in three or five years. Staying as we are is not an option. We must start now: get marketing itself as the commercially invaluable asset it should be and change the story.

I do not have a crystal ball, but I know what happened when commercial landscapes changed dramatically in the past. In a recession, companies start looking at reducing costs, and the first to go are departments that don't contribute to revenue. If there is pressure on margins, an organisation will chop one side of its sales generation coin before the other – I don't think I need to spell out which side. And when a smaller business gets merged or acquired by a larger one, economies of scale dictate that obsolete functions are disposed of or swallowed up by the buyer's existing teams. The only chance for any department to survive in these circumstances is to make itself indispensable to the revenue and big picture strategy.

Redefining marketing for the modern world

As I write this book in the latter half of 2021, the global economy is suffering. Consumer confidence is at a low ebb, and the repercussions of the pandemic are likely to be with us for many years to come.

Our internal research shows that more than half (53%) of senior marketers have suffered budget cuts since the virus outbreak, while 43% have experienced a headcount reduction. Nearly seven in ten marketers are now required to prove how they deliver return on investment, and 24% report this as critical to the ongoing existence of the marketing department. By default, this sort of pressure forces most marketers into a panic where they start to shout about vanity metrics (likes and sign-ups) even louder, rather than working on the things that actually build the business in the long term. In some ways, this reaction is understandable because time is not on their side, but that is my point. Let's start readdressing the balance and fixing the problem now. As we have discussed, big creative ideas and brand building are the activities that underpin turning lower funnel conversions and conversations into sales. You cannot get to the bottom of the funnel without addressing the top.

According to the Institute of Practitioners in Advertising, brands that invested in growing excess share of voice (ESOV) by over 8% during the 2008-9 downturn grew their market share by an average of over four times more during the recovery phase. So, in an era of budget cuts and short-termism, marketers must continue a long-term approach to measurement to safeguard the future of their brand and department. And this is impossible unless the board recognises the value of their marketing departments and trusts them to deliver results that count.

The best time to plant a tree was twenty years ago; the second-best time is now

Those numbers indicate a cycle that for too long has seen marketing teams rely on arbitrary and siloed metrics they believe superiors want to see to prove their strategic worth to the board. And it's a problem that was bubbling under the surface long before COVID-19 reared its ugly head. If anything, the pandemic has simply accelerated the inevitable path marketing has unknowingly forged for itself.

I am a bit of a technophobe but also a realist, and I believe the future of marketing depends on the intelligent use of these ever-evolving technologies. But the explosion in digital-first marketing and measuring its impact using sophisticated MarTech tools also means there is nowhere for marketers to hide. The problem is that boardrooms don't generally understand the true value of marketing and certainly not of creative marketing. So they have no choice but to place a lot of emphasis on the numbers and tangible metrics (that don't relate to business outcomes) to rate the performance of their marketing function.

The ever-decreasing circle needs to stop because marketers have distanced themselves from metrics like revenue and gross profit and obsessed over vanity metrics like click-through rates and conversions for far too long. And this puts the problem back at the marketing department's front door on both counts. As I have shown in earlier chapters, the only way to survive is to convince the board they are providing a return on investment and then use that licence to get back to creative-first marketing.

An old Chinese proverb states: the best time to plant a tree was twenty years ago; the second-best time is now. Twenty years ago, I barely knew the difference between sales and marketing, and I certainly didn't understand the complexity of the situation marketing finds itself in today. Looking at it now, from my senior position in a marketing agency surrounded by a team of seriously smart marketers, it is clear to me that the problem started long before I arrived on the scene. It has been a slow shift of focus, and the irony is that digital technology is both at the heart of the problem and probably holds the keys to the solution. But the main change needs to start in the hearts, minds and ambition of today's marketers – both the leaders and the new blood entering the profession. And it must begin today: tomorrow at the latest.

Start building a strategic marketing hub in your business

As I have mentioned already, I am not suggesting every marketer reading this book must aim for the boardroom, as there can only be one CMO or CRO in each company. But every board-level marketer will need a team of business-savvy marketers or revenuists to support them and help drive change. So there is no place to hide. Recent research from executive recruitment firm Spencer Stuart shows just twenty-six of the thousands of public company board seats are occupied by CMOs – that number must change.

Iris Meijer, CMO at Vodafone Business, has earned a respected voice in her organisation by being commercially minded. As a result, her team is currently spearheading one of the company's three strategic pillars. She says, *"Marketing departments and leaders have always held central importance to the business, now more than ever. One of the reasons for this is there's a plethora of actionable data available, enabling us to make strategically informed decisions. I truly believe the board is beginning to recognise this".* She explains, *"Marketers must gain confidence in their ability to use this data in a way that will meet business objectives and position themselves as custodians of the customer. A good place to start is developing closer relationships with the sales team and getting involved in more commercial decisions".*

Raja Rajamannar, Global Chief Marketing and Communications Officer at Mastercard, points out, *"It's not just marketers who can benefit from marketing owning a seat at the table. Other board executives will benefit by learning how to evaluate and squeeze the most out of the function".* He says, *"The only way a business can differentiate right now is through marketing, and if companies want to do that, they need to have a marketing perspective on the board".*

Rajamannar also serves on the board of the Ad Council, business services company PPL and private healthcare business Bon Secours. He highlights additional board positions as opportunities that enable marketers and their organisations to shift marketing priorities in line with business strategy. *"As a marketer, it gives me a different take on how the board thinks from a governance perspective, among other things. I can also sit there and pull the attention back to the consumer; it's hugely helpful. And when I go back to my day job at Mastercard, I know how the vortex works, and I can be a much more efficient executive committee member who can represent the marketing interests extremely well."*

Being on the board or simply having a respected voice gives marketers a long-term opportunity to educate stakeholders around the table about the longer-term impact marketing provides. Being in the room enables marketers to identify and understand the metrics that actually matter to the business and gives them a forum to reinform key board-level stakeholders who have previously misunderstood the significance of their department.

Marketers are the primary brand custodians in their organisations, making them one of the major influences to lead generation and filling the sales pipeline. I repeat: marketing as a critical function of modern business must change, and there is not a minute longer to lose in starting the ball rolling. I sincerely hope this book has given you something to think about and, more importantly, some strategies and ideas you can take and use to instigate change and ensure your future. And if you have read this book, with a nod of agreement, thinking how you already knew all that, I hope you pass it on to someone else; because I guarantee you will know someone who needs to learn.

In the final chapter, I will share one of the most recent parts of my personal business story to date. How we took a service that evolved out of Raconteur's publishing business into a fully-fledged marketing agency and completely rebranded our agency business as alan.

Sharing this latest chapter of our story is not a vanity metric; it is a practical example of a creative-led marketing strategy being deployed as a commercial solution to a situation we faced in our company.

CHAPTER 20

A case for change:
alan. who?

In chapter fifteen, I told the story of my journey from arriving in London and taking on my first sales job to becoming the CEO of alan. agency. I even shared the embarrassingly costly magazine failure that still haunts me every time I think about the lack of vision and foresight that allowed it to happen. In this final chapter of my book, I want to back-peddle to the accidental birth and slow development of the business that became alan. over five years. And in a similar way that Bene helped me explain the process of bravery in the B2B marketing model in chapter fourteen, I want to demonstrate this as a case study for rebranding a business by discovering the solution. This has so much relevance to the overriding topic of this book because creativity and the science of solving problems may seem complete opposites but are essential marketing skills drawn from the same mould. And when you approach your personal evolution and commercial development (as a marketer) in the form of a problem to be solved, you can start to unleash your creativity.

Although I'm aware I covered some of our background story in chapter fifteen, I want this to be more of a standalone case study, so please forgive the repetition! Raconteur has always been known as a highly reputable publishing house, and, around 2015, several large organisations like Schroders, KPMG and Deloitte approached us to ask if we could create reports, like the ones we did for The Times and The Sunday Times, under their brand styling and guidelines. So, we started this new service in a *similar*...yet completely different way to the traditional publishing arena that we originally called Custom Publishing. The more bespoke work we did, the more some customers asked us to provide other specialist marketing services. Almost by accident, this arm of our business transformed into a fairly comprehensive all-service marketing agency. After a short time, it became clear that the obvious thing to do was create a clear distinction between the two sides of the business from the publishing side of the company. Initially, all our business came from existing customers and contacts approaching us because they were involved in us delivering the service in the first place. Our problem came when we started to pitch for new opportunities, with other companies, through tenders and RFPs. Whenever we found ourselves in front of a new customer, ready to pitch for their business, the same questions would come up, and we found ourselves spending ten minutes justifying ourselves even being in the room. It would go something like, *"We know Raconteur, you are a publishing company. What are you doing here?"*

The issue was: externally, there might not appear to be much difference between a custom publishing service and an agency, and as sister services, publishing and marketing agencies are well aligned and complementary. Yet, the two services are entirely distinct in terms of the way they deliver results and are worlds apart - for our customers and us.

Publishers exist to create relevant, engaging, readily available and highly consumable content. They can consistently target their own audience and sell creative advertising solutions to brands who want to get in front of that regular readership. By its very nature, it's quick, effective, sharp, and (usually) a shorter-term approach. As a publishing house, Raconteur had, over the years, garnered an extremely positive reputation as an independent publisher.

In comparison, an agency takes a longer-term, hand-holding, relationship led approach. The goal is to provide highly consultative, long-term, strategic advice to our clients. The best marketing agencies typically become ingrained in their clients' culture, brand, story and communication of its values and message (internally and externally). The approach is always 'needs first' rather than 'audience first'.

While we were happy to explain the difference, prove our expertise and demonstrate what we could do, it became more of a barrier than a foot in the door. Even when we rebranded to Raconteur Agency, the same thing happened more often than not, causing much frustration.

Although that didn't stop both divisions from growing year on year for six years in a row, we were sure there would come a time when that stopped, and we increasingly realised we needed our customers to recognise how our service differed from Raconteur. So, in 2020, we decided it was time to rebrand the agency business away from the Raconteur name completely. That process instantly highlighted another issue that almost made us rethink before we even got started. The one thing being called Raconteur did for us was buy recognition, kudos, track record and familiarity. Although humbling to recognise how much gravitas the Raconteur brand had accrued, that first hurdle took far longer to get over than it perhaps should have done. But once we had taken our bravery pills, we returned to the obvious conclusion that a new identity needed to be uncovered and presented to the world.

Uncovering the enigma and cracking the code

As with chapter fourteen, I have relied on our Creative Director, Benedict Buckland, to help me explain the following thinking and the process behind the discovery and development of the brand we ultimately uncovered. Once we had fully decided to pivot the business by creating a standalone brand and learning our lessons from the magazine debacle, we started with a strategic research project. It is always profoundly more challenging to apply to yourself the things that you do well for others because it becomes personal (perhaps even paranoid). So we worked very hard to avoid any predetermination of the direction we followed. We did this by starting with independent data and views from three perspectives: external client interviews, analysis of our competitors' proposition, and discreet internal employee surveys and focus groups. In essence, we wanted to establish what we thought we did, what we wanted to be, who our customers thought we were, what they perceived as our strengths, and what they and prospective customers wanted from us.

Once we had this clarity of need, we worked through the process we consistently applied to our own customers until our new identity emerged. One of the themes that consistently materialised in all three areas of the research was the idea of providing solutions. Our employees faced challenges and situations they didn't know how to solve and the subsequent thrill and satisfaction of working out how to do it. Discovering the solution to a seemingly unfathomably problem and bringing it to life in a creative, innovative and adventurous way was what drove the people who worked for us and gave them the most job satisfaction. I suppose it was a bit like the feeling a bunch of geeky scientists might get after sending a snowball into hell and bringing it back home safely.

The clients we were already working for gave similar feedback regarding our creativity and eagerness to experiment with new concepts, but their main comments were around reliability and trust. You see, it is all well and good expressing the ideas and concepts of a brand, campaign or marketing idea, but does it deliver results? As discussed throughout this book, most marketing people (agencies and internal teams) think purely about marketing as 'the thing they do', but the people who run the businesses and pay the bills want outcomes. When a company employs a marketing agency, they do not actually want marketing guidance from that agency: they want a definite, measurable, provable return on investment. Interestingly, some of our clients hadn't even fully identified this clarity of thinking until we pointed it out to them. In essence, they were looking for a solution to their biggest commercial problem: how can our marketing help generate more direct revenue and sales opportunities for our business?

The competitor analysis looked at the proposition and positioning of other agencies. And while some did appear to be focusing on the bigger picture rather than selling a list of marketing services, none had fully captured the essence of marketing as a problem-solving function in their own branding and message. So, when we assessed all our research together, it quickly became apparent there was convergence around this idea of clearly identifying the end goal and coming up with a solution. The word 'solution' didn't really fit the description or appeal of a creative agency narrative yet seemed to describe a consultancy business and echo that sort of terminology. But everything still pointed towards coming up with answers to unsolvable problems, and we could not ignore what our extensive research had told us. So, we invented a process to try and discover our own meaning and understanding of the concept. What did 'solving our clients need for a return on their marketing investment' really mean, and how could we reinterpret that in terms of a creative expression of what we deliver?

Looking back to the bravery in the B2B marketing model I described in chapter fourteen, we carried out extensive research and developed a version of our DNA. Our customers wanted us to solve their need for marketing to support their sales effort and help them generate more revenue, and we loved the challenge and buzz of uncovering and implementing big ideas that delivered those outcomes or results. We had also looked closely at the audience we worked with and the kind of customers we wanted to work with in the future. Clearly, we needed to target people and businesses who understood the need for revenuist marketing, not just marketing as a function. Unless our customers recognised they needed a solution to their revenue-generation gap, there really was no point in engaging with us as a partner. We had now arrived at the 'identify the intersection' stage of the model. And we had to discover the place where those two elements of the puzzle converged.

It sounds simple to state the final outcome, but believe me, a lot of intelligent discussion, working late, and sleepless nights went into composing our strapline: B2B Marketing. Solved.

Noel Gallagher, of Oasis and High Flying Birds fame, says of the creative process of writing songs, "Songwriting is like fishing - and me, along with people like Paul McCartney, Bono and Chris Martin are all fishing in the same river trying to catch the great ones". He quotes Keith Richards of the Rolling Stones as saying, "I believe all the songs are already there, fully formed, and you just need to find them", and how Neil Young describes it as "Waiting by the rabbit hole, ready for the rabbit to stick its head out and being ready to catch it". In his fishing analogy, Noel says that he keeps fishing because he wants to make sure he gets the best songs before the other great songwriters snap them up.

We felt that we had really identified a unique perspective on something clearly already there when we arrived at that creative expression of 'the thing that we love to do and that our customers need from us'. The simple, direct construction of those two short sentences, as well as the words themselves, perfectly described the outcome we wanted: resolving our clients' problems by delivering the results they need. With an acronym, two words and two (extremely important and 100% relevant) full stops, we had arrived at our solution. The full stops represent the definitive resolutions we deliver, and the words explain how and who we work for. So we now had our articulation of the creative idea in a meaningful strapline.

The final part of the journey was a place most people try and start. Hopefully, by now, you can see why that approach is back-to-front, simply because it ignores the value and purpose elements of finding a complete marketing solution. So we started asking ourselves how we could develop a brand name to reflect the idea of problem-solving within a B2B marketing context. We went through all the typical processes involved in working through a creative process, including thinking of analogies, metaphors and various synonyms around problem-solving.

As you can imagine, there were many contenders for the title, and some of them were incredibly creative and almost caught our collective heart. In a few instances, I know several team members were quite reluctant to let go of various themes, but we were looking for the perfect solution, and it had to be right on every level. So, while there were lots of good suggestions and many came close, for the sake of honesty and full disclosure, there were also loads of rubbish suggestions. And we deliberated over them for hours: in the office until midnight, at the pub, on Zoom, and far too many 5 am text messages. But even among the good ones, nothing seemed to fully encapsulate the coinciding science and art of problem-solving or the combination of left and right brain thinking we wanted to capture.

Heading down this avenue, we decided a historical figure with a story to tell might hold the answer and eventually, we arrived at the door of Alan Turing. After all, he represents the definitive problem solver of his generation. He was instrumental in solving one of humanity's greatest challenges, morally and intellectually, by cracking the impenetrable enigma code and beginning a chain of events that would defeat the evil cloud closing in on the world. And beyond the most famous of his achievements, there lies an equally impressive body of work that demonstrates his ingenuity, creativity and robustly logical thinking. His personal life (the tragedy and longer-lasting legacy of equality beyond his years) also spoke volumes about his influence on the world. I would also like to state here in print – for the record – that we arrived at the idea at least a year before the UK Royal Mint or the Bank of England chose to put his picture on the latest fifty-pound note!

We all loved the idea of using Turing as our central theme, but as with all creative work, the initial inspiration needed some tweaking and cosmetic adjustment before it was ready to go to market. Phonetically, the word Turing was awkward, and visually the appeal didn't ring true either. And we also didn't feel it would be right for our business to become defined or limited in scope to an individual person's identity. We were convinced by the inspiration of what Turing achieved and stood for, but we wanted to represent that idea on our terms, in line with our own sense of purpose and meaning as a problem-solving marketing agency. This process also clarified that we didn't want our brand to describe a traditional English first name either, so we chose to display the word in a more mutable form, with lowercase lettering and a defined full stop at the end representing the definitive solution.

So at the end of an intense, comprehensive (brave and creative) marketing exercise, our brand profile became defined as...

Name: alan.

Strapline: B2B Marketing. Solved.

Value proposition: Ingenious solutions to complex B2B marketing problems. Guaranteed.

Purpose: To move marketing forward.

Promise: Impact.

How we do it: We tell it like it is. We ask what if. We always work it out. We guarantee results.

Brand narrative: Solve problems. Move forward. Have impact.

The video on the front page of our website sums up the story perfectly: https://www.alan-agency.com/

And with that summary of how our business applied the fundamental principles of marketing the bottom line to ourselves, I want to finish this book with a challenge.

What are you going to do (not what can you or what would you like to do) to change your personal brand, positioning, voice and influence on the world of marketing? Between 1942 and 1945, Alan Turing and others solved a problem that played a pivotal role in ending World War Two. The bottom line is that their efforts probably saved hundreds of thousands of lives. A few brilliant people made a massive difference.

Your role as a marketer might not save lives. But it can change the course of your company's future, ensure your colleagues' job security and livelihoods, and create a fulfilling and rewarding career to support you and your family for life. And, if you really apply yourself, you can master the Marketer's Hierarchy of Needs and become a famous marketer operating at the very top end of the bottom line.

The ball is in your court. Marketing is about making things happen. What are you going to do?

ABOUT THE AUTHOR

Richard began his working life, age 16, serving tables and behind the bar at a holiday park in the New Forest. He quickly recognised that becoming memorable to guests would earn him more tips. One such incident, a favourite with diners and involving a bottle of tomato sauce (read the book to learn more!), got him noticed by the park's new boss. It was ultimately also responsible for him cancelling his university plans. Instead, he became his boss's protégé, gained an Open University degree and embarked on a speedy climb through the ranks and across all the park's departments.

When his boss made a throwaway comment one day, Richard realised it was time to move on. That comment? "Rich, you've gone all pipe and slippers." He was 21 and had reached the ceiling in that business.

He quickly secured a role with a high-ranking London publishing firm. Soon after starting, he realised he hated all that firm stood for and quit to join Raconteur, the renowned City firm that provides high-quality content for The Times, Sunday Times and top B2B brands like Google, Deloitte, Dell Technologies and more.

A few years later, he became Raconteur's Commercial Director, before becoming MD of alan. Agency in 2020 and CEO of both alan. and Sectorlight Marketing (both part of The Raconteur Group) in 2021.

As a former salesman, he has seen firsthand the disadvantage businesses put themselves at by failing to get sales and marketing to collaborate. Like many salespeople, he'll confess, he wasn't always a fan of marketing in his early career. But - unlike many salespeople - he soon realised the skills are complementary. Winning campaigns happen when both sides work together. This is why collaboration between sales and marketing is the key theme of his first book.

If you're wondering whether such a crazy business life has room for a personal life – yes, it does! Richard is engaged to his partner of 6 years, Bethany and the proud father of his 1-year-old cockapoo, Rory. He is an avid Arsenal fan and loves to holiday in the sun... as much as his schedule allows.

Lightning Source UK Ltd.
Milton Keynes UK
UKHW020343030222
398099UK00001B/12